MW00881438

I know nothing but …

Helen Eltzeroth

Copyright © 2015 Helen Eltzeroth

All rights reserved.

ISBN-13: 978-1508768449

ISBN-10:1508768447

DEDICATION

This book is dedicated to my children, Jo, Shelly, Becky, and Jake, who are not only my children, but also my good friends. They helped make me the person I am and continue to strive to be.

It is also dedicated to my niece, Teresa, who I took care of when she was a little girl and who became my unofficial daughter, always sharing her infectious smile and laughter with others.

CONTENTS

FOREWORD

When I was a child, we lived in a small town near a big park. With four children, my mother knew the value of providing outlets for childish energy, so we often went hiking in this park. A special tree grew along one of the trails, a tree grown into a funny shape with a strange root formation that created a loop of living tree that one could crawl through, if one were both relatively small and so inclined. My mother was both.

Objectively, it was a ridiculous thing to do, to go for a hike along a particular trail just so we could crawl through an oddly shaped tree formation, yet we were endlessly charmed by this activity as children. I didn't realise at the time just how unusual it was that my mother was charmed by this activity as well. She didn't get belly down in the dirt and crawl through a loop of tree trunk because she was in any way humouring us; she had genuine enthusiasm for a simple but slightly weird way of having fun. For me, that sums up her life philosophy: don't pass up a chance to do something fun, even if you look slightly ridiculous in the process.

I've followed my mother through lots of figurative tree tunnels, long after the last time I followed her through the actual tree tunnel. She's a role model for a lot of people, me included. I could list lots of reasons she is inspiring: she was a success in the financial industry at a time when such success was VERY hard for women, let alone women with children; she lives and acts on her integrity, rather than just talking about it; she provides unflinching and unwavering support for her family and friends. These are all both noble and true. And she talks about some of these things in this heartfelt book.

But the most inspiring thing she's done? That still has to be crawling through an odd tree tunnel, delighting herself and saying more clearly than words could that life is to be seized with both hands, while laughing as much as possible.   *Written by Jo Eltzeroth, Dorking, Surrey, U.K, March, 2015*

PREFACE

I began this book more than fifteen years ago as a way to share some thoughts with my children and friends. It was always a work in progress and over time, I thought it lost its relevance. But when I read it again at the beginning of 2012, I realized that many of the things I had to say and many of the issues I discussed may still have relevance. So … I finished what I started.

The book is divided into three parts – Part I - Community, Part II – You, and Part III -- Me. In the first part of the book, I discuss how the communities in which we live help shape and change the values we embrace. In the second part, the issues discussed are more personal and focus on issues that help define who we are and whom we can be. I share stories from my early years throughout Parts I and II because I believe stories can shed light on the influences our backgrounds have on the values we adopt.

The third part is my life story and focuses on the people and experiences that were the framework for the person I sought to become and the foundation for the person I am.

Although you may not share any of my views, perhaps reading about the issues and stories I share will serve as catalysts for you to tell your own stories and motivate you to examine your own views about today's issues. No doubt, some of you may disagree vehemently with my views, and that is fine. My intent is to stimulate the discussion – not to effect agreement or disagreement.

I am not a writer or a philosopher, but I like to think there is a bit of teacher in me who wants every person to stretch to be everything each can be. I hope the issues discussed will be relevant to those reading about them today and just maybe to those who may read about them in the future. Life is the gift but how we live it is the adventure.

That is my challenge and my dream.

PART I --COMMUNITY

CHAPTER 1 – ORDINARY PEOPLE

The opinions of great men and women are recorded in essays, books, biographies, and autobiographies. But where are the thoughts of ordinary people like my grandmother or your grandmother recorded? Could this knowledge help us understand how the social norms in our own time came to be? Oral histories that record personal stories through interviews have been around for a long time; and although they are often available in museums, they are not part of the formal history that is taught to our children. If more of us encourage our parents and grandparents to tell us about their customs and values, perhaps we will grow up with stories to share that will help a broader audience of future generations understand how the past helps shape the future.

It is popular in today's political environment to highlight an individual or family that supports the politician's position or legislation he or she supports, and the media is eager to include these stories in press releases, columns, news analysis, and opinions. It appears that politicians and news analysts know what we have not realized yet – we want to know about

> ## A STORY
>
> My brother (he was my half brother because my Mother had been married before she married my Dad) was in the Navy, and I remember him coming home from the war. It was near Valentine's Day, and my sister Sharon and I woke up to big hearts filled with candy on our beds. He also bought a car – which made him seem rich since my Dad didn't have one. I don't know how old Joe was then, but I idolized him – he was my big brother!

"ordinary" people. We want to hear their stories.

I have a document written by my great, great uncle about his father. The love and respect he felt for his father was moving and seemed to represent a much gentler time - a time when families were the primary influence on people's lives. Perhaps my great, great uncle's writing motivated me to write about the importance of preserving the relationships formed in families and in sharing the values they held. Portions excerpted from my great, great uncle's writing follow.

Writing from Sylvanus Barrett in summer of 1924:

"…I think I knew my father better than many sons know their fathers. My recollection commences in 1863 when father was in the vigor of mature manhood. I assisted to my utmost strength and ability to help him make a pleasant, healthy home out of those heavy timbered swamps, labored by his side and know the iron a man had to have in his soul to face it with a smile. He was not all the time able to keep the smile on the faces of his boys, but it seemed to be eternal with him, and I haven't a doubt that he is smiling in his sunny way in eternity at this minute. I was associated

A STORY

I was named after my Dad's sister, my Aunt Helen. For my graduation from high school, she paid for me to come to visit her in Los Angeles, CA. My friends drove me to the airport in Chicago, and it took about as long to drive to the airport as it did to fly to California. We got lost several times. The plane I flew to LA in was a constellation, and it took roughly 6.5 hours to get there. I flew back on a jet; jets were just becoming widely used for U.S. passenger travel. It was a magical trip for a little girl from Indiana. My Aunt worked for the LA times, and she introduced me to the Manager of Saks where she purchased a mink hat. We went to the Moulin Rouge, the Spanish area of LA, the Brown Derby, and many other famous places. It was a trip that I still remember vividly.

with father for many years after I grew to manhood. He was not strong as some as a financier, but he was industrious and honest and I do not believe he ever complained or became discouraged if finances were not as successful as he had expected. He was deeply religious but was liberal and charitable toward the views of others. When he fell asleep December 24, 1906, the thought of his weakest and youngest son was that he beheld the end of one of God's noble men."

Every time I read this writing, I am humbled by the simple and honorable way my ancestors lived. When I compare their times to mine, I realize how much easier daily living is today. But the most important impact this writing has on me is the admiration and respect a son had for his father. I know this is just a small glimpse from the best of my past, but it helps me understand and appreciate where we have been and gives me an example of one man's respect for another that I will not forget.

But the past does not always show us the right way; sometimes it shows us the way not to go. There were practices and attitudes that I am ashamed of from my grandparents past and from earlier years that I remember. I am appalled at the social acceptance of some of these -- racial prejudice is the most offensive, but there have been others. I remember my dad bringing a live chicken home from the store, and my sister and I watching, without any thought for the humane treatment of the chicken while my dad chopped its head off. We watched and counted how many times the chicken flopped in the backyard after its head had been cut off. How barbaric

A STORY

We lived a few houses down from the local grocery store – Happy Owens Grocery Store. Happy had a delivery truck that he used to deliver groceries, and we children always wanted to go with him and ride in the truck. I was only around 4 or 5 years old, and I wanted to go with him one day. He asked me if I had asked my mother if I could go. I lied and said yes, but I hadn't asked her. When we came back from making the delivery, I found out that the neighborhood kids had told my mother that I ran away down to the creek. She was always afraid of one of us drowning so I was in big trouble. She had been looking everywhere for me. I don't remember her being mad at Happy, but if she was, I probably wouldn't have known about it. I am quite sure she was not happy with me though!

-- now I am appalled, but back then, it just seemed "normal." This acceptance of an inhumane practice helped me understand how prejudice and social behavior can persist, unless we stop to think about the things we do, the way we live, and the way we treat each other. I also learned that often people don't behave a certain way because they are trying to be unkind, cruel, or condescending to others -- they are behaving in a manner consistent with how they have been taught. If a southern gentleman opens a door for a liberated female, is he being condescending or displaying the manners he was taught? Will the liberated female take offense because she was not taught the same manners but was taught to do things for herself, including opening doors? Both of these people may be behaving in the ways they were taught and not seeking to offend the other.

For most of us, there are few glimpses into the thoughts that motivated our ancestors. But I suspect there's a lot we could learn if we had their stories to read and share.

> **A STORY**
>
> We lived next door to a restaurant, and the owners had a little boy named Jerry Allen. I was in the first grade, and I was asked to watch him so I played with him in a fenced in area of the yard. He had a pet rabbit in that fenced in area. One day Jerry Allen was chasing his bunny around the yard, and he caught him … almost. He stopped abruptly holding the rabbit's tail in his hand! He held it up (he was around 3) and said fix it. I did what any five-year old would do – I ran to get his mother for help.

I hope that by documenting my thoughts and telling some of my stories that others will do the same – both formally and informally. I will share a few of my stories throughout this writing -- to practice what I preach! (See "A Story" sidebars)

Perhaps the views of ordinary people can provide the understanding that will help future generations take the good from the past and replace the bad with the better, but without anger toward others who come from different social backgrounds with different social practices and customs. Life is not black or white, but a combination of black, white and gray. So are my thoughts.

We are a society composed mostly of ordinary people like you and me. The famous people will be remembered, but they make up a small percentage of our society. The ordinary people are and can be exceptional and need to be remembered and valued for what they can teach us. It is not what we do that determines our worth but how we live our lives.

A STORY

My sister and I had the measles at the same time. This was before a measles vaccine was available, and we more or less expected we would get measles. We were put together in one bedroom that Mother kept dark by keeping the light off and the blinds down. She brought us our meals, which we ate in bed and bathed our rashes with a warm solution of something that made them feel better. I don't remember it being a particularly bad time, but then I was only six!

CHAPTER 2 – HISTORY AND STORIES

History books describe major events and the famous people and trends that contributed to the events, but they do not generally include stories about ordinary people. "Do not confuse efforts with results," seems to be our guideline. Events record the results, but the essence of life for most of us is in the "struggle." Where are the struggles, the failures, the successes, and the thoughts people had in everyday living recorded in history?

We analyze and "presume" what contributed to the events in history, but this seems particularly arrogant to suggest how people felt, without having first-hand information. Which comes first – the thoughts and then the event? The event and then the thoughts or are they intertwined.

A STORY

One of my favorite memories is going to the movies with my Mom, Dad and sister. We didn't have a car. My Dad rode a bike to work, and we took the bus to the movie theater. I remember walking happily to the bus stop with my family and coming home from the bus stop with my Dad carrying me. I was only about 5 years old so I probably couldn't stay awake that long. Most often, the movie was a cowboy movie. There were no R rated movies then.

My daughter Jo said I couldn't tell her how to feel when she was only 16 years old, and she was right. A black man in one of my college classes tried to explain how he felt, but the class argued with him because he "shouldn't" feel the way he did. But he did. History should include these feelings – a child from a divorced family in the 70's, a black man from a Midwestern inner city in the 60's – they all contribute to our history and help explain why people behave a certain way.

History is generally taught from an academic perspective, or at least the "mainstream" seems to come from that perspective. Should stories about the lives of ordinary people be included in history books, or should they be for entertainment and an informal means of communicating life lessons? How do children hear stories – do they hear them from their parents or hear them through mass media? When I was in grade school, we played with children from a Greek family in our neighborhood, and we were very curious about how they lived. The mother frequently told a story about a little boy named Tommy, which gave us a glimpse into Greek life and values. We felt we were special when we were included in this family time. We loved listening to the stories.

But what are the influences on the stories mass media produces? Have we narrowed our scope of stories to those that the masses will watch or read? What is the love affair that we seem to have with reality shows? Some of us love them, while others think they're stupid. Do we become arrogant or defensive because the representations in these shows don't fit our backgrounds? Why not tell your own stories to your children in addition to those told to the masses. If the stories we tell are of true-life events and family values, does this help or hurt children's understanding of history if it is not consistent with mainstream stories?

A STORY

I remember sitting on the chair in our kitchen, smelling the lilacs from the lilac bushes that were right outside the windows. Mother had painted the kitchen table and chairs white and put decals on them. This was customary at the time. The kitchen was a happy place. But it wasn't quite so happy when I hooked my feet around the legs of the chair and fell off, hitting my eye on the corner of the stove. This was my first black eye! But I would receive two more before I was seven – one looking up for a softball I had hit, and another when I sneezed and hit my head on the corner of the sink.

I include a story about my Grandpa and Aunt Mame (see sidebar), but I did not realize until my Aunt Mame died that she was my grandfather's common law wife. My grandmother had died in childbirth, and her sister, Aunt Mame, moved in to take care of the other children. I did not think anything was strange about going to Grandpa and Aunt Mame's house. I just accepted it as normal; and the rest of the family must have as well since I was 17 years old when I learned the facts about their relationship.

The stories I share in this book are of a more naïve time when children were allowed to be children and were more accepting of relationships and circumstances. Today a story about a common law wife would not be

> **A STORY**
>
> My sister and I used to walk to Grandpa and Aunt Mame's house to play poker with matchsticks and to fight over who got to put the ice card in the window for the iceman. I still remember that card; it was an octagon-shaped orange card. When the iceman saw it, he would stop at the houses with cards in their windows and bring in ice blocks for their "iceboxes." Yes, it was called an icebox then because that was what it was!

particularly relevant since people live together who are not married but who are in a committed relationship. People living together are part of the mainstream today, but the reasons they live together are not normally to take care of a sister's children.

History books describe events and generally describe the effect on the main stream of society or highlight a particular group that changed society. But where can we learn about the accomplishments of the people who didn't achieve anything great but who built the stepping-stones for others to follow? You don't have to be famous or be at the top of the field in whatever work you do to be great. Who provided the influences for those people who are at the top? Who taught the child to love to read? Who taught a daughter that integrity was not negotiable like my father did? My father was a man of tremendous integrity. He was a Supervisor in a factory – a blue-collar worker, but he taught me values that I will always have. Everyone was welcome at our house, but he expected people to be respectful of others while there. He taught me that your word was not to be compromised. We can learn about our parents' times through history, and if we're lucky through stories. My father's influence on me is part of my history.

But today generations often use new and different communication methods to learn about history. Technology has provided multiple ways for instant communication – cell phones, text messaging, Facebook, Linkedin, Twitter, Instagram, etc. Older generations did not grow up with computers, and many are not comfortable with today's technology options. Party lines and letter writing are unfamiliar forms of communications to younger generations, but various forms of instant communications are. So the challenge for all of us is to understand that different ages may communicate differently, but how they communicate is not a value judgment about the person communicating. How then does this affect history and our ability to tell stories to future generations? Ereaders such as Kindles have changed how we read and even learn so should we adopt a new way to share family stories or is it important to retain the social interaction that in-person storytelling provides. I am part of the older generation, and I like the sense of family and connection that is provided by face-to-face storytelling. Am I just being old? I have

A STORY

My friend Terry and I (both 5 years old) saw this beautiful new car parked in front of our house, and we decided to make it even more beautiful. We spent all day painting it with mud. We lived near a factory, and apparently, the owner worked in the factory, and when he got off work and came to get his car, he saw our handiwork. I heard him talking to my mother and realized he didn't think it was beautiful (although I had no idea why). I was scared so I locked myself in the bathroom by putting the hook in the slot. But I couldn't reach it to unlock it when my mother told me it was okay. My dad came home from work and crawled in the bathroom window to get me out. While I learned that painting a car with mud didn't really make it pretty, I also learned I could count on my parents to be there for me even when I was bad.

embraced all the new technology and have an iPhone, iPad, (old iPod), and utilize email, Facebook, Linkedin, text messaging, streaming video, etc., but I still love getting a personal handwritten note or spending time with family or friends reading a book out loud. Is there a way to preserve the gift of stories to describe the past from ordinary people in a way that is appealing to all generations? Perhaps multiple venues for storytelling are the answer, but just like James Russell Lowell's poem. "...the gift without the giver is bare." The story without the teller may be bare as well.

A STORY

My mother used to read me a story from the Bible every night. I don't know why she chose the Bible because we didn't go to church then, and I didn't consider us a particularly religious family. I wanted the same story every night – the Christmas story. She read it so often that I can recite it still ..."And there were in the same country, shepherds abiding ..." It was a special time that I looked forward to with my Mother.

CHAPTER 3 – OPPORTUNITIES

Two of the issues that are often discussed by politicians, funders, and others are "Equal Rights and Equal Opportunities." I realized when I reread what I had written about these issues that I didn't really understand what both meant, and I suspect I am not alone so I spent some time doing a little cursory research. I found the following legislative documents applicable to these issues and include excerpts below. (This is not a comprehensive list, but it should provide some background to frame the discussion.)

- [1] The Civil Rights Act of 1964, which provided for Title I – Voting Rights, Title II – Injunctive Relief Against Discrimination in Places of Public Accommodation, (without discrimination or segregation on

A STORY

When I was 13, my Mother, sister and I all worked at a restaurant by our house. The restaurant was also right beside a factory so customers were mostly factory workers on lunch breaks. My Mother and sister worked the counter, and I was the dishwasher – the kind of dishwashing machine was me – manual with dishes in large baskets transported from sink to sink. I loved being able to earn a little money to buy clothes and to go to movies.

---

[1] "Transcript of Civil Rights Act (1964)." U.S. National Archives & Records Administration. July 2, 1964. Accessed January 15, 2015. www.ourdocuments.gov/doc.php?doc=97&page=transcript.

- the grounds of race, color, religion, or national origin) Title III, Desegregation of Public Facilities (equal protection of the laws, on account of race, color, religion, or national origin), Title IV – Desegregation of Public Education, (without regard to race, color, religion, or national origin), Title V – Commission on Civil Rights, Title VI – Nondiscrimination in Federally Assisted Programs, Title VII – Equal Employment Opportunity (without discrimination because of race, color, religion, sex or national origin), Title VIII – Registration and Voting Statistics, Title IX – Intervention and Procedure After Removal in Civil Rights Cases, Title X – Establishment of Community Relations Service, and Title XI – Miscellaneous.

- [2]National Council of Women's Organizations, ERA Task Force, The Equal Rights Amendment: Frequently Asked Questions, "Women shall have equal rights in the United States and every

> **A STORY**
>
> In my high school, the kids who were bound for college could take College Preparatory English with the assumption that others didn't need that level of education. Even though I wasn't headed for college then, I could dream, and I took the class. (I didn't go to college until I was in my mid-twenties.)
>
> Similarly, Latin was the only foreign language taught at my school, and there was a waiting list to take the class. I was not at the top of the waiting list, and I never had the opportunity to take it. (I had always gotten good grades and was in the National Honor Society, but I didn't have the money to be college bound or at that time, see it as an opportunity.) I assumed my role would be to grow up, get married and have kids!

---

[2] Francis, Roberta W., Co-Chair, ERA Task Force. "National Council of Women's Organizations, The Equal Rights Amendment Frequently Asked Questions." August 1, 2014. Accessed January 16, 2015. www.equalrightsamendment.org/faq.htm.

place subject to its jurisdiction. Equality of rights under the law shall not be denied or abridged by the United States or by any State on account of sex."

- [3] The Proposed Equal Rights Amendment: Contemporary Ratification Issues, "Congress could revisit the contending points raised by different analysts if it considers legislation that would seek specifically to revive the proposed Equal Rights Amendment, or to accept the additional state ratifications."

The two words "rights and "opportunities" are frequently used interchangeably, but in reviewing the legislation, equal opportunity specifically refers to Title VII – Equal Employment Opportunity, which insures equal employment opportunities without discrimination because of race, color, religion, sex or national origin. The other titles to the act prohibit discriminatory practices based on race, color, religion, or national origin, but not sex. Although equal rights are insured by the Civil Rights Act (1964) without regard to race, color, religion or national origin), I think many still feel we have not achieved this, as it relates to sex, unless we enact the Equal Rights Amendment.

> **A STORY**
>
> In grade school, girls were not allowed to wear pants to school so we (my friends and I) decided we should protest by wearing our fathers' ties to school. Although we were protesting against discrimination against us because we were girls, we did not think about Women's Rights or Equal Rights. We were just addressing a problem we saw in our little school in the early1950s.
>
> This practice of prohibiting girls from wearing pants to school continued until my children were in grade school – when that policy was finally changed.

---

[3] Neale, Thomas H. "The Proposed Equal Rights Amendment: Contemporary Ratification Issues." Congressional Research Service. April 8, 2014. Accessed January 16, 2015..www.equalrightsamendment.org/misc/CRS%20ERA%20report%204-8-14.pdf

The proposed Equal Rights Amendment proposes equal rights for women. Although I have been a supporter of the Equal Rights Amendment, I have not given the same attention to the circumstances in which I might not have equal rights that I have given to equal opportunity in employment. I think woman have felt inequalities more visibly in employment. I know I have. I remember being asked whether I planned to have a family in an interview for a job right after I graduated from high school. Much later when promoted to a new job after college and having children, I was asked whether I'd be able to travel because I had children. (I was a single parent and sent on a weeklong trip after moving to a new city with four children.) So, I felt the inequality in employment practices and felt I had to prove myself by being better at the job than my male colleagues are in order to get ahead. But I have felt less valued as a female at other times too, for example, times when conversations were directed to the male with me while ignoring me. Is how we treat women a result of custom

A STORY

When my sister and I were in high school, we didn't have money to spare to buy our lunches so my Dad would take his lunch hour from his job at the factory and stop by high school to pick us up to go home for lunch. It was cheaper to prepare cooked lunches like macaroni and cheese than it was to buy sandwich material.

This may have been just a particularly tight time for us because I only remember doing it for a short period of time. But I don't remember minding it – I thought we were fortunate to get such good lunches. I credit my parents for making us feel that it was special.

and social practice and not a result of our value system? Although we still do not have legislative protection for equal rights by sex, perhaps the proposed amendment will be passed in the near future to put what many of us think is inherent in our values as a nation. But equal opportunity presents a different dilemma.

We have legislative support for equal opportunity, but how it works in reality and what we think it means is a bit more disquieting. Many of us use equal opportunity to suggest that every child should have an equal opportunity to become an attorney, and we think it means that. But does it? We also say every child should have equal opportunity for an education and through education, each can accomplish whatever he or she dreams. In reality, this often means daddy or mommy write checks for tuition for the wealthy to go to college or to take crash SAT courses, while the poor have the opportunity (if they are exceptional) for a scholarship, or if they don't mind going in debt for their future, to obtain a college loan. How is this equal opportunity? What will the history books teach children about this equal opportunity? Will they show the struggle of the exceptional children to achieve goals that are harder to obtain because they are poor? Some have mother's like mine who took in ironings to give her children the opportunity to participate in after-school activities. Others have parents who "do without" to save money for their children to go to college. Still others give their children the opportunity to learn determination, integrity, loyalty, and respect by modeling these behaviors. What do these struggles teach our children about opportunity in a way that it can be applied to their lives? The children we rear are our responsibilities, and some of the opportunities they have are within our control. We don't all have the same opportunities to give, but we can give them

> ## A STORY
>
> The first telephone service I remember was one that we shared with three or four other families. It was called a Party Line. We had to wait our turn to use it, but as kids, I don't think we were as polite as we were supposed to be. When you picked up the phone, more often than not, one of the other parties would be talking on the line. The telephone was not a major source of communication then. People visited each other in their homes, grocery store, church, and at community events.

the best we can offer. My father told me that I could try to do anything I want, and I believed him. He gave me his view of equal opportunity, which meant I saw all doors open. He didn't have the opportunities that money would provide, but he had the opportunities that belief could provide. I believe that opportunities cannot all be legislated. We ordinary folks have to contribute. The great folks contribute to the legislature and the big changes, but we ordinary folks contribute to the very hearts of our children. Equal opportunities can be found in material things, but they can also be found in the values and views of our parents. There will always be those who have more and those who have less than we do, but what we do with our very individual opportunities, is the challenge.

CHAPTER 4 - HOME

The process of achieving home ownership can be different because of the difference in opportunities we have. Those who come from a sound financial background have the money for a down payment or the home can be a gift from a wealthy relative. Others with limited income can save their money and buy a lower-priced house with a government-insured or guaranteed loan. Is the American dream of home ownership in tune with the needs of today's society? Is the American Dream a holdover from earlier times when owning land was the only way to achieve status and benefits? Is it still true in some jurisdictions that you have to be a homeowner to serve on a jury? If not, it hasn't been that long ago when it was.

We place value on home ownership and reward those who achieve it by giving income tax deductions (for borrowing the money to buy a house), provide government-insured or guaranteed loans, and provide tax credits for energy-efficient improvements to our houses. In the past when inflation was high, many people made money on their houses and were able to move up to a more

A STORY

As a teenager, I didn't think my parents knew much about anything. I thought I knew everything! I remember most evening meals sitting around our red Formica top table with my Dad saying, "Sit up straight, keep your elbows off the table, don't shovel your food, don't talk with food in your mouth," etc. At the same time, my Mother was trying to get me to be quiet by kicking me under the table.

expensive house or were able to build equity as a future investment. This is not true for many of us today. Inflation in many areas has not increased enough to cover the transaction costs of a real estate sale. Moreover, today, the mortgage market has many home values underwater caused by the volume of foreclosures resulting from the economic recession experienced the past several years. Although this is changing as the real estate markets recover in many areas, real estate as an investment in our futures is not a sure thing.

Why is home ownership preferred to renting? Because it shows stability? Because it shows a savings pattern? Stability may not carry the same weight or more specifically, be related to a specific location, as it once was. Now many of us will have several jobs before we retire. No longer is the trend to stay with one company or even within one locale. So why do we insist home ownership shows stability when in fact, it often creates hardships and losses for those who are more mobile because of a changing job culture.

Encouraging saving is even more interesting when analyzed as a reason to

A STORY

My paternal grandfather contracted tuberculosis after his wife died and was sent to a sanatorium in California to get well. When he was released, he came to live with us, but my mother was terribly afraid that he wasn't really well and that we children would be infected. (I had scar tissue on my lungs), which made her more afraid. So, my father found a Rooming House not too far from our house for my grandfather, and he stopped most every day on his way home from work to see his father. My grandfather died when he was living in the Rooming House, and I remember seeing a couple of older men who had apparently been his friends at the Rooming House at his funeral. I had never been to his Rooming House, and I'm not certain I knew what a Rooming House was.

support home ownership. During the past thirty years, many of the initiatives to provide home ownership opportunities by both the government and the private sector have been to reduce the amount of the down payment required to loan money to buy a home. Lower down payment requirements, assisted down payments through gifts and subsidies, and multiple borrowers are some examples of the affordability initiatives. Little to no down-payment programs have historically characterized government loan programs. These programs make saving less of a requirement to achieve home ownership.

The reason many people want to own a home is to achieve a certain amount of independence or autonomy from being at the whims of others. We want to control our environment and be a part of the society of the "haves" because home ownership is one of the things "haves" enjoy. We are not a homogeneous group of people in the United States, and we are much more mobile than we were 25 years ago. We are also becoming older as a population. Some of us live in cities, some in suburbs, and some in rural areas; but we try to impose the same housing needs on all. Some of us will live in several different geographical areas to be close to our jobs, and many of us will not be

A STORY

One of my favorite things to do when I was in grade school was to play in the coal bin. We had a coal furnace in the basement. I would slide in through the window where the coal was delivered. Then I'd spend hours playing on the coal. I had no idea that this was not good for me. I also don't know if my mother knew I was playing in the coal bin or if I got in trouble for doing it. I just remember it was fun!

able to afford or want the burden of upkeep on a house when we retire. So why does "renting" a home mean you are not part of the American dream? Perhaps we need to examine the rental structure to bring more independence and autonomy to this form of living, rather than to continue to perpetuate a "dream" that has lost some of its meaning. Why judge people as successful or unsuccessful based upon whether they own their own home? Why reward people through government programs and incentives based upon whether they own or rent their homes. I suggest that the home ownership transaction is so encumbered with people and firms that make money from it that it has become "sacred" in our society, not because it is socially important but because it is economically important to so many. The fees and costs are overwhelming. You may have a real estate agent, perhaps two, a real estate broker, perhaps two, an appraiser, a surveyor, a pest control firm, a home inspection firm, a home warranty firm, a water analysis laboratory, an attorney or settlement firm, a credit reporting agency, a loan originator or mortgage broker, a lending institution, a secondary mortgage market firm, a private mortgage/government insurer or guarantor, a title company, a hazard insurance company, document preparation software or firm, a tax service firm, and a flood certification service. This list does not include builders, developers, contractors, and others involved in the new

> ## A STORY
>
> My Uncle Clyde worked at a printing press in our downtown area, but he couldn't walk properly, and he rode a bike everywhere he went. We were always very excited when Uncle Clyde came riding up to our house with his dog, Spot, to visit. I guess in today's culture, he would be looked at as having a disability, but back then, he was just "Uncle Clyde."

home industry, nor does it address in each of the firms the people involved, who are commissioned or who perform overlapping services. Most of the services are directed toward protecting the investment quality of the loan for the investor but do not necessarily provide value to the homeowner Not nearly so many are involved in an unsecured transaction, and an unsecured transaction is generally considered more risky. The argument for protecting the creditor's risk for residential properties is that by making the market more efficient (and less risky), we create more opportunities for people to buy homes by making more funds available -- particularly in capital short areas. But does everyone need or want to own a home? Can we achieve independence and autonomy by renting a home? We lease cars, and apparently, it is a good idea for some but not all people. Why isn't renting a home a good idea for some without relegating them to the "have nots?" Are we spending and rewarding ownership so much that we've overlooked home living? Shouldn't we begin to look at renting as a more viable option for some in highly populated areas, those with jobs that are more mobile, those who are retiring, and perhaps others who like the flexibility of changing residence more often than once or twice a lifetime? Why build more retirement and suburban communities? Why not examine our rental housing market and find ways to be creative and adaptive to our changing social needs? Doesn't home-ownership as currently rewarded by society perpetuate the haves and have-nots? If you grow up and work hard, you can own your own home! Owning may not be better for all our lifestyles, but it does not mean that being a renter should mean you are an underachiever, under saver, or under anything. Let's look at what makes sense for our changing society and not perpetuate the class system that it seems to support. We ordinary people have been taught that owning a home is the goal to which we should aspire. When I was growing up, we lived in two rental houses and then

> **A STORY**
>
> It was a clear snowy night, and the streets were icy. We had moved to our new house in the west end, but we still missed going to the local grocery store by our old house so this night, Mother, Daddy, my sister and I walked and slid down the streets to "Happy Owens" store. The snow came down in big flakes, which were reflected under the streetlights. My sister and I ran ahead and slid back to Mother and Daddy, laughing all the way. It was a magical night with lots of laughter and a warm feeling of being together as a family.

two houses that my parents purchased. The two rental houses were just down the street from each other, and I never knew why we moved. Since it was in the same neighborhood, it did not present any social problems for me. My friends were the same.

The first house my parents bought was clearly a step up in neighborhoods – we moved to the west end, and although our neighborhood was not affluent, we were adjacent to one that was. Then we moved a little more to the outskirts, and the house was not as nice as the first one. The first one had hardwood floors, a full basement, and a nice backyard. The second house had tile floors and no basement. Both had the same number of rooms and were about the same size. Our friends were determined by the neighborhood we lived in, and the first house introduced us to a more "haves" neighborhood. The second house was not quite so influential, but because we were in high school by then, we already had a base of friends from the old neighborhood.

Had we stayed in the two rental houses, the activities I participated in would likely have been different because I would have been with a different group of friends who didn't aspire to go to college or to become professional workers. Most were children of blue-collar workers, and assumed they would also become blue-collar workers. While what people do does not define who they are, how renters looked at opportunities

A STORY

My older teenage sister Betty had a boyfriend who owned a Model A Ford that had a Rumble Seat in the back. A Rumble was on the back of the car, where a trunk would be today. When it wasn't open, it folded down into the car. We felt very special if we got to take a ride in the Rumble Seat.

and how home owners looked at opportunities were different because of what was normal in the neighborhoods.

My parents gave me the intellectual and emotional view that I could do anything, so even if we had stayed in the rental properties, I think I might have still felt I could do whatever I wanted with my life. But perhaps others would not. I don't know …

Ordinary people can be rich or poor, but where they live can have an influence on their children's lives along with the values they teach them. Moreover, whether we are property owners or renters should not affect how we are viewed by society or the opportunities we believe we can pursue.

CHAPTER 5 – INSTITUTIONS AND RULES

<u>Institutions</u>

In our not too distant past, we put people with mental conditions in insane asylums because we did not have a way to care for them, except to isolate them from the larger society. We also put children without parents in orphanages. We did not have the infrastructure of social services, foster parents, and adoption opportunities that we have today. We sent poor people to poor farms because we did not have a social network designed to take care of them at the time either. Today, we often segregate older people into retirement communities and assisted living facilities because we are still working on figuring out the role of older adults in society. We are living longer and healthier lives, which has brought more attention to "being older" by society in general and by older adults particularly. Living longer also means that many are living with chronic health conditions, and although there is a movement for older adults to be cared for in their homes and communities, it is not the general practice,

> **A STORY**
>
> The house I was born in (in a laundry basket) had an L-shaped front porch. It seemed very big at the time, but when I went back to see it years later, it was really quite small. One of my fondest memories about that house was mother making homemade chocolate fudge syrup and all of us sitting on the front porch eating ice cream covered in the fudge syrup. Ice cream came in rectangular containers back then so it was sliced, rather than scooped, but the important part of the treat was the fudge syrup!

and institutionalization is still more customary for older adults with chronic health conditions.

These practices suggest that society has historically segregated people who are different from the currently defined norm. I use the term currently defined purposefully because I believe we continue to see changes in what is currently defined as part of the main stream. For example, black people, Asian, Hispanic, American Indian, physically challenged, mentally challenged, women, children, mentally gifted, old, orphaned, poor, rich, sick, criminally associated behavior, diseased, and even the physically elite, have all been subjected to segregation. While we recognize that our society is not homogeneous, we strive for homogeneity to develop norms. Today, there are programs that integrate physically challenged children in traditional schools. On the other hand, we frequently segregate ourselves by economic and cultural means, sometimes by choice, but other times because of inadequate opportunities. I don't know whether these initiatives confirm that

A STORY

Mother grew corn, tomatoes, and strawberries in the backyard of the house we lived in until I was about six. She may have grown cucumbers and green beans, but I remember the tomatoes, corn and strawberries the best. We used to pick the tomatoes off the vine and eat them while they were hot from the sun – they were delicious! She also grew rhubarb beside the house and made rhubarb pie. Everyone seemed to have these Victory gardens then even if they had very small yards. This was during the early 1940's when everyone had ration books, and the food that we grew helped us supplement the food that was scarce through rationing.

involuntary segregation is more a result of economic disparities or whether cultural bias still plays a role. In many communities, we can find neighborhoods that are primarily Hispanic, Asian, Russian, Korean, etc., but are these neighborhoods formed by choice? Similarly, are our institutions developed based upon economic issues, lack of options, or choice? Understanding segregation and integration in our communities may be the precursors of changes that will redefine how and why we establish institutions in our communities. How should our educational programs be designed? Are traditional schools no longer the cornerstone of education? Are rehabilitation facilities and nursing homes no longer the best way to care for people with chronic physical and mental conditions?

We are afraid of what we don't know, and institutions, in my view, have provided a place to put people with conditions or qualities that we haven't figured out how best to handle while we search for better options. Institutions are temporary solutions. Mental institutions, orphanages, poor houses, and perhaps now traditional schools and nursing homes could be examples of institutions that have served their purposes and now must change.

We choose institutions, based, in part, upon the communities in which we live and the level of financial solvency we enjoy. Many

A STORY

I remember when I was in grade school being lined up on one side of the room and instructed to walk to the other side of the room with my feet straight ahead. Apparently, being pigeon-toed was unacceptable, and the school took it upon itself to correct children who walked pigeon-toed. I didn't question why I was told to do it. I just did what I was told. I'm not sure it worked. I still walk a little pigeon-toed.

of our ancestors had multiple generations living in one household. This may have been more prevalent in farm households since it meant more people were available to help with farm chores. Many Native American households often include multiple generations as well. These practices are likely a result of custom, economics or both. The economic strength of the household contributes to the options that the household has to deal with new situations – a parent with dementia, a physically or mentally challenged child, loss of parent who provides the primary earning, etc. Further, there may be differences in the quality of the institutions based upon the neighborhood or community in which they are located. Moreover, people living in rural communities may not have convenient access to institutions of any type. The time has come to re-examine the role of institutions in our communities. Is there a better way to care for people who have different conditions and characteristics – what do you think?

Rules

Rules are tools we often use to preserve our institutions and social practices. Rules tend to standardize behavioral patterns and make behaving differently less likely. In some cases, the rules we live by suppress creative thinking and in my view, have not always served the common good of society. For example, in the 50's, girls couldn't wear pants to school. And some institutions have assigned seating for meals. Why?

Is there a different way? Sometimes I don't know why I so blindly accept rules, but I most often just follow the rules that are stated. Appointments can only be made between the hours of 9:00 and 12:00; proper attire required; ring the bell; take a number, three people abreast, no standing, do not fold,

> **A STORY**
>
> The day my parents brought home our first TV was memorable. It was black and white and had rabbit ears on top. We didn't get an antenna on top of our roof until later. We had to get up to turn the TV off and on since we did not have remote controls, and only a few programs were available at that time. But that first day, we carried the kitchen chairs into the living room with our popcorn and watched Wrestling, Roller Derby and "Uncle Miltie," Milton Berle.

and my favorite, "stay on the line and your call will be answered in turn." I don't want to stay on the line. I want to talk to someone. That's why I called. I didn't call to stay on the line so I could be transferred through a series of options to leave a message.

Our children are probably subjected to rules the most – by everyone and every place – parents, schools, theaters, athletic events, and most organized events they attend. Granted, many rules do serve a safety purpose but many also serve as a convenience for those in charge. How many of us rebel in following directions to put something together or in reading a computer manual to find out how to do something in a software package? Instead, we try it ourselves first. If all else fails, read the manual. We want to think on our own, creatively, but we (society) continue to make it easier just to conform. "Dare to be Different!" Lace your shoes backwards. Sit down on the elevator. Pay by check in a cash line. Don't write your telephone number on your check. Do get out of your car and watch the sunrise, a deer, a bird, a flower. Do take time to sit down and listen to a friend, a child, or a stranger, even though you'll be late for a meeting. Do smile and laugh even when others may think being reserved is more appropriate. Do not be afraid "to be" even when rules or custom discourage you.

We grow up in different geographic areas and in different socio-economic neighborhoods. What may be "normal" behavior in a middle class neighborhood in a small town may not be "normal" behavior in an upper class neighborhood in an urban area. Some social "norms" seem to become rules and others do not. For instance, I was taught to stand when an older person entered the room. Some were taught to give up their seats on a bus or subway for an older person or a woman. Others were not. Are these just manners and not social norms? Do rules ever reflect social norms? Or, are rules adopted primarily for safety, economic reasons or to facilitate an activity

A STORY

When I was in grade school, I wanted to be the smallest girl. We thought you would be popular if you were little and petite rather than tall and slender. We were always lining up for something, and I was happy when being little put me at the front of the line.

I was small and young (5) when I started first grade. Kindergarten was only for those who could afford to pay for their children to attend. Perhaps I wasn't quite ready because I forgot how to count between the first and second grades. I still remember how I counted – 1,2,3,4,5,6,7,8,9,10,11, 12,13,31,32 …

I'm sure today that this would be explored to see if there was a physiological or psychological reason causing my memory loss. Back then, it wasn't, and I remembered how to count without any assistance…umm

– raise your hand to speak, go to the microphone, submit your questions in writing prior to the event, etc. Do we lose sight of the needs and desires of ordinary people when establishing some rules? Do we stifle creativity with others? Do we think about the effect some rules have on people -- particularly those in institutions? For example, meal times in nursing homes – although some have begun to offer some flexibility – most are still fairly rigid. Do bathroom breaks really need to be scheduled?

To Recap

The social norms ordinary people grew up with affect the impact that institutions and the rules established by the institutions have on them. Some may "feel" they cannot deviate from the rules and thus lose their ability to think and feel creatively. Others may feel comfortable to just accept them as guidelines and not feel inhibited by them.

In the past, people assumed they would take care of their older relatives by caring for them in their homes. This was the norm, but with an ever-changing society, this is no longer the "norm." People live longer. People no longer work at the same company for their entire lives – whether blue collar or professional. Transportation options provide opportunities for people to move and work in different geographic areas. This makes caring for family members in our homes more challenging, especially since most older adults want to live in their own communities as long as they are able. No one wants to spend his or her last days in a nursing home. No matter what age, being close to family is

> **A STORY**
>
> Alleys were the place where I spent a lot of time playing when I was a child. In fact, I still have a scar and a piece of cinder in my knee from a fall I had at a very young age. One of our favorite things that took place in the alley was when the Rag Man came down the alley with his horse. We ran to follow him to where he took a break and tied his horse under a tree. We wanted to pet his horse. We didn't think about what he did with the rags or whether he was collecting them, selling them, or both.

important to most of us, regardless of our mental and physical conditions.

We are in a new age of electronic communications, and enhancements in scientific and medical technology force us to look at traditional ways we've done things. We have new capabilities. Our institutions and the way they are operated will likely be influenced by economic and scientific concerns as well as by moral and social values. But it seems clear to me that today's technical and economic environment provides an opportunity to reexamine our institutions and rules and ensure they consider human values and our different and changing lifestyles.

It is apparent that institutions and rules are established for a variety of reasons — our changing needs, safety, economic considerations, efficiency, and more. Ordinary people have an opportunity to influence how institutions are utilized and which rules are

> **A STORY**
>
> One of my Mother's constant requirements was that we dress warm so we wouldn't catch cold. I always seemed to have a runny nose as a child. So, she made us wear knee socks to school. I hated them so as soon as I was out of view of my house, I would roll them down. This probably contributed to my getting more than my share of colds. But when we did get colds, Mother would grease our chests with camphor oil and put a flannel cloth over it under our pajamas. I still remember how good it made me feel. It was almost worth catching a cold so I could get this treatment.

appropriate and which are just an unnecessary convenience. One way to do this is through the examples we set for our children and neighbors. Choosing to keep older generations at home when possible, providing caregiving as a choice and not a burden, setting household rules that stimulate independence along with safety (not children should be seen and not heard), and modeling behavior that is open and receptive to new ways of doing things are just a few examples of such behaviors.

PART II – YOU

CHAPTER 6 – UNIQUENESS

There are many physical, emotional, and environmental influences that contribute to making us unique. While I believe that our behavior can be attributed to them, perhaps there is something else that is the center of our actions and the centering point for us – our souls. I realize there is an abundance of scholarly discussions about why we behave one way or another and whether or not we have a soul, but I want to pose an introspective discussion based upon what you believe, which I hope will motivate you to examine what you think makes us unique. Different words often mean different things to different people; and for the purpose of this discussion, I list definitions for a few relevant words from the Oxford English Dictionary online. See below.

[4]**Soul -- noun**

1The <u>spiritual</u> or <u>immaterial</u> part of a <u>human being</u> or <u>animal,</u> <u>regarded</u> as <u>immortal.</u>

[5]**Genetics -- plural noun** *[treated as singular]* 1The study of <u>heredity</u> and the <u>variation</u> of <u>inherited</u> <u>characteristics.</u>

---

[4] soul. Oxford Dictionaries. Oxford University Press.
http://www.oxforddictionaries.com/us/definition/american_english/soul (accessed March 12, 2015).English

[5] genetics. Oxford Dictionaries. Oxford University Press.
http://www.oxforddictionaries.com/us/definition/american_english/genetics (accessed March 12, 2015).

[6]Physiology -- noun

1The <u>branch</u> of <u>biology</u> that <u>deals</u> with the normal <u>functions</u> of <u>living</u> <u>organisms</u> and their parts.

1.1The way in which a <u>living organism</u> or <u>bodily</u> part <u>functions</u>: the physiology of the <u>brain</u>

[7]Perception -- noun

1The <u>ability</u> to <u>see</u>, <u>hear</u>, or <u>become</u> <u>aware</u> of something through the <u>senses</u>: *the normal <u>limits</u> to <u>human</u> perception*

1.1The state of being or <u>process</u> of <u>becoming</u> <u>aware</u> of something through the <u>senses</u>: *the perception of pain*

.2A way of regarding, understanding, or interpreting something; a mental impression:

[8]Behavior -- noun

1The way in which one acts or <u>conducts</u> oneself, especially toward others: *good*

1.1The way in which an <u>animal</u> or person acts in response to a <u>particular</u> <u>situation</u> or <u>stimulus</u>:

1.2The way in which a natural <u>phenomenon</u> or a <u>machine</u> works or <u>functions</u>:

[9]Belief

1An <u>acceptance</u> that a <u>statement</u> is <u>true</u> or that something <u>exists</u>:

---

[6] physiology. Oxford Dictionaries. Oxford University Press.
http://www.oxforddictionaries.com/us/definition/american_english/physiology (accessed March 12, 2015).
[7] perception. Oxford Dictionaries. Oxford University Press.
http://www.oxforddictionaries.com/us/definition/american_english/perception (accessed March 12, 2015).
[8] behavior. Oxford Dictionaries. Oxford University Press.
http://www.oxforddictionaries.com/us/definition/american_english/behavior (accessed March 12, 2015).
[9] belief. Oxford Dictionaries. Oxford University Press.
http://www.oxforddictionaries.com/us/definition/american_english/belief (accessed March 12, 2015).

1.1Something one <u>accepts</u> as <u>true</u> or <u>real</u>; a <u>firmly</u> held <u>opinion</u> or <u>conviction</u>:

1.2 A religious <u>conviction</u>:

[10]**Unique – adjective**

1Being the <u>only</u> one of its kind; unlike anything else:

[11]**Genetics --** The study of <u>heredity</u> and the <u>variation</u> of <u>inherited</u> <u>characteristics</u>.

<u>Genetics</u>

Genetics are often credited with being the cause of why we have certain physical characteristics and why we may be predisposed to have certain diseases or physical conditions. Genetics may also account for certain behaviors. Perhaps the scientists have known this for a long time, but it makes me think how much more influential genetics may be when I observe two of my children's behaviors. My daughter, Becky, behaves very much like her Grandma Reder in one particular respect. She wants what she wants right now, and this was one of my Mother's most endearing behaviors. The family immediately attributes this behavior to both Mother and Becky. When Becky was a young adult, she did spend some time around Mother, and some suggest she may

---

A STORY

One day my Dad went swimming with my sister and me at the local swimming pool. I was the swimmer in the family and had the local pool record for 11 and 12 year old girls 50-yard freestyle, but my Dad was the real swimmer in the family. He had been a merchant marine and was used to swimming in the ocean. What was uncanny was my stroke was very much like his. He didn't teach me how to swim, and I had not seen him swim until then.

He threw my sister and me in the water at the diving platform in the deep end and almost got us kicked out of the pool. It was such a fun time, and we loved it that he almost got us kicked out!

---

[10] unique. Oxford Dictionaries. Oxford University Press.
http://www.oxforddictionaries.com/us/definition/american_english/unique
(accessed March 12, 2015).

[11] genetics. Oxford Dictionaries. Oxford University Press.
http://www.oxforddictionaries.com/us/definition/american_english/genetics
(accessed April 16, 2015).

have acquired this behavior by example. Why that particular behavior? My son, Jake, has physical mannerisms, for example, how he looks at you, and social behaviors, always drawing people out and encouraging them to tell him about themselves that are characteristic of his father. What makes this uncanny is that Jake did not grow up with his father and has not spent the amount of time with him that is normally associated with acquiring behavioral patterns. Are both Becky and Jake's behaviors and mannerisms primarily a result of genetics? Only Jake's? Neither? Are genetics the only thing that makes us unique? What do you think …

Physiology

Our physical bodies react to substances and hormones in ways that can be observed in how we behave. Can these substances and hormones also result in how we feel? We seem to accept that hormones do. The brain as well as other body receptors, e.g., skin can "perceive" invasions to our bodies. Similarly, the physical body can "speak" through its reactions to physical stimulus as well as through traditional forms of communications, such as speech, written language, mathematical symbols, and musical compositions. The body communicates

A STORY

I worked in a department store when I was in high school. This was before the days of high-speed elevators. In fact, we had an elevator that was operated by a man or woman who sat on a stool beside the door. When you entered you were asked, "What floor please." It was a more personal experience than what we have today. Of course, we only had a couple of floors in the department store building.

emotions or perceptions of circumstances -- often by position. For example, fear can be shown by lowering one's position. Dogs generally show fear in the same way. Acknowledging being bad or ashamed is also shown in similar ways by dogs and humans -- lowering the head or eyes. Happiness is shown by increased activity or vibrancy. This too appears true of dogs and humans. Anger can result in raised voices and raised positions for both dogs and humans. While I know there are studies that address whether dogs have

35

emotions, and some suggest that my comparisons are invalid. But for the sake of this discussion, let's say these are just observations about similar behaviors. For humans, these behaviors have become somewhat traditional ways of communicating – bowing, shaking hands, standing, and sitting. I wonder, however, whether all of the behaviors that appear to be the result of physiological responses are always the results of only physiological influences. There was a story about Aaron Ralston, an American outdoorsman, who amputated his own hand and forearm to free him from a boulder that he had been stuck in for several days. If this was indeed true, his action seems to be in opposition to how he would react physiologically and perhaps there was another influence... What do you think?

Perceptions

If our physical bodies respond to stimulus – both physical and mental, are there other influences on our thought processes and the choices we make that we don't always acknowledge. Do our perceptions, whether accurate or not, play a role? For example, a dog who grew up in a fenced yard doesn't perceive he can jump the fence and get out because he couldn't when he was a puppy. How is this different from a young black person born in the inner city who doesn't perceive that he will get out because he couldn't as a child? We could infer then that our perceptions can be influenced by the environment in which we live and by the

> **A STORY**
>
> I purchased my first car for $100. It was a 1948 Ford Coupe. We didn't have Driver's Education at school, and for some reason, my Dad didn't teach me how to drive. So, my friend, who had a 1937 Plymouth and her license, and I took the car out on the country roads. She played with my radio, trying to get it to work while I learned to drive.
>
> When I took my driving test, my car wouldn't pass the requirements so I borrowed my sister's car. I had to use hand signals for turns then since turn signals were not standard. My car was manual steering but with three on the column instead of on the floor. I loved my 1948 Ford, and my friends preferred to take my car instead of the new Buick that one of my friend's had.

education we receive. A low-income physically challenged person living in an urban setting may not perceive his or her opportunities the same way that a high-income physically challenged person living in a million dollar house does. Do perceptions combine with other factors to influence our thinking, our beliefs, and our decision-making – in other words, our uniqueness?

Belief

We all seem to want to belong to or believe in something. How else do we explain the popularity of reality shows, game shows, government run lotteries, etc? We want to believe there is a gold pot at the end of the rainbow. We want to believe that there is a way to improve our present situation. We want to believe there is life or something after death. We want to believe that we will someday understand our purpose or the meaning of life. I think I fall into the class of many of us -- believer. I believe in fairy tales -- I want to. It makes me feel better to do so. I believe in Santa Clause. I believe in the goodness that these tales represent. I believe in the goodness in life and in people.

> **A STORY**
>
> My Mother was a small gentle woman, but she didn't tolerate anyone messing with "her man." One Friday night, Mother called Phyllis, my sister, to come down to the corner bar. Mother thought another woman was flirting with my Dad. Although she had gotten rid of the woman for the time being, she wanted reinforcement. So Phyllis went to the bar and sat in the booth with Mother and Dad to discourage any further access to my Dad. Dad loved all this!

All of these beliefs reside in what I look to as my centering point, my soul. We are all unique; we have different brains, hearts, lungs, bones, muscles, etc. Some of us develop our muscles through training. Some develop minds through training. Some develop both. Some of us have many environmental influences. Some have few. Some of us are believers in many things. Others find it difficult to believe in things they cannot see or that are not scientifically based. I cannot see my soul, and I cannot comprehend what a soul is, but I believe I have one. Do you believe you have a soul?

CHAPTER 7 -- SOCIAL PRACTICES

I discuss social practices in this chapter rather than social values because our social practices do not always reflect our values if the value has not been embraced by the majority of people. When I was a young working mother, I was not able to take sick leave to stay home with my children or even to have a child. I suspect, however, that if you asked anyone at the time whether family was a value they embraced; the answer would be yes. You could then argue that family, as a value was not reflected in the social practice in the workplace. This continues to evolve in the workplace today, but I suggest there may be other social values that are not reflected in our social practices, either in the larger community or for us as individuals. We may say we value our elders, but do we show that value when we make fun of them or talk to them in a condescending manner.

An example of a social practice that does not have support by some that has been in the news recently is that of vaccinating against measles. This raises the question of individual freedoms but also of the danger that not vaccinating imposes on others. The practice of vaccinating against measles in the past had not been elevated to discussion in the daily news because there had not been a recent outbreak of measles in the U.S. The outbreak of measles that started in Disneyland in California that spread to other states, making the issue more of a concern. There are those who suggest legislation, and others who argue for the individual's right to choose. I wonder whether these individual social practices can be resolved so that they are supported by a majority of the larger community. Our social practices are and should be subject to examination as we continue to understand each other better and are open to different views. You could argue that a woman's right to choose is another social practice that is not supported by all. In fact, how the discussion is phrased is different by those who take different views. It is frequently framed as a right to life by some, and as a woman's right to choose by others. This issue is part of the broader discussions about women's rights and religious convictions so there are confounding factors surrounding this social practice discussion.

In addition, the social practices we adopt are often grounded in a specific time and can be incorrectly interpreted if taken out of the context in which they were adopted. Judging yesterday's behavior by today's social norms can produce criticisms and a misunderstanding of the intent of the practice and the people who adopted them. Perhaps this is the reason there is so much controversy about latent memories and their effect on the individual today. Earlier, I described a practice of cutting a chicken's head off and watching (as a spectator sport) while it flopped around without its head. While I am abhorred today at this behavior, I wasn't at the time, and I do not feel that my Dad was a bad person for doing it. It was a past behavior that was accepted at the time, but was changed as people came to realize there was a better and more humane way to kill the chicken. Similarly, when I was in grade school, it was not unacceptable to paddle children. I did not say, beat children. People who used this form of discipline thought they were paddling them to teach them that their behavior was unacceptable. While we children did not want to be paddled, most didn't view it as scarring us for life or as something barbaric. Today, we do. We have learned there are better ways to guide behavior, but most of us that grew up in a time when paddling was an accepted practice, were not psychologically hurt by it. It was a normal social practice, and looking back through psychoanalysis **and** suggesting there was more to it might lead to misinterpretation of the circumstances in which it was employed.

A similar parallel can be drawn if we try to use yesterday's social norms to judge today's behavior. How many of us have heard, "In my day..." Those who grew up in a loving environment when paddling did not mean you didn't love a child but was a way to teach proper behavior may suggest paddling is acceptable today without understanding that today's children consider it abuse. And today's parents consider it unacceptable and even criminal. However, the elder population that vocalizes this view may only be expressing how they were socialized without realizing how inappropriate it is for today's behavior, particularly when the abuses in the past led to inflicting pain. Abuse was unacceptable then and now. I'm not sure how we make certain we only keep the good from the past and discard ideas and behaviors that are harmful to others. Perhaps open minds to change and to the examination of the intent and consequences of social practices will lead to social practices that benefit the community and the individuals living in the community.

Unfortunately, often we don't make the changes that are needed to some social practices until we hear about the abuses of what was thought to be an acceptable practice. We didn't think … particularly if it didn't affect us directly. Often it takes too long to wake up and realize that the social practice is not a good one, and we need to be a more thoughtful society in looking at our social practices to ensure all are served equally and no segment is harmed. It took us much too long to recognize that a predominately-white society's treatment of Black people was horrific.

Our debate over affirmative action is perhaps an illustration of two different possible consequences of a social program. Affirmative action was designed to correct a social injustice -- discriminating against a category of people. While eliminating discrimination and creating equal opportunity is desired, is discriminating through affirmative action programs the best way?

Who is to be selected for college admission if a Black female and a White female are equally qualified in every aspect? With affirmative action, no matter which choice is made, discrimination can be argued. If the Black female is chosen, the White female can argue that reverse discrimination against her exists. If the White female is chosen, the Black female can argue that she was discriminated against because she's Black. I don't pretend to know the answer, but it does make me think.

We can see a similar example when we look at a practice that most of us have either practiced or experienced. If we tell a child to behave as we tell them because we are the boss or if we show the child how to behave by example, which do you think will be more easily accepted? Animals learn from their parents by example. Can we be good animals too?

It seems when we try to legislate or force social behavior before it is accepted by the larger society, generally, we are not successful. Prohibition is an example. Social legislation sometimes raises our consciousness about our freedoms even if the intent is to correct an injustice or in some people's opinions, be better for the greater good.

▶ STORY◀

My sister and I were sitting in the restaurant where we worked with our co-workers, and somehow the discussion of Black people sitting at the back of buses came up. Both my sister and I said we didn't think it was right, but an older woman in our group yelled at us and told us we were "blank lovers."

We lived in a small town in the Midwest, and my sister and I had very little interaction with people of different races. But our Dad was always welcoming to anyone at our house, regardless of color, so this must have been where our beliefs came from. I have to confess: we had never really stopped to examine the practice of Black people sitting at the back of the bus. At the time, it didn't seem to affect us personally so we were oblivious to just how wrong it was. We should have been "thinking" more, even though we were just teenagers.

Presumptions. Presumptions often direct some of our political actions. Those inside the beltway often presume the rest of the country feels the same as they do or have the same needs and beliefs. While these presumptions may be based upon a political sampling, we know that we can spin the results of statistics to support our views. In the United States, we presume our beliefs and values can be incorporated into one practice for those living throughout the country in different states that may have customs and practices that are different and unique to their states. Is this always realistic and desirable?

I frequently tease my sister, Sharon, for her presumptions. For example, she presumes people will want to give up the good seats they purchased at the theater to move over a couple of seats to allow her group to sit together. Her presumptions are that people want to be helpful and kind to each other. Other presumptions we sometimes have aren't so positive. We presume that people in the company of documented bad people are bad. In fact, our legal system supports this negative presumption by its treatment of accessories to criminal acts. Similarly, our legal system presumes a person is innocent until proven guilty. However, from my limited exposure to the system, it seems that reality is the other way around. Jake's (my son) traffic citations were handled in a manner that assumed he was guilty. If you look at the number of cases that are plea-bargained, doesn't this process also presume guilt? Or has this practice evolved to facilitate gaining information that will help with another crime or for economic reasons because of tight budgets? I don't know.

Our mainstream educational system presumes all children are ready for certain types of learning at pre-established ages. Although there are innovative programs and accelerated and remedial classes for some, these are for the exceptions, not the norm. We presume age predicts readiness. On the other hand, perhaps standardization just makes a structured educational program easier to manage. But what are we giving up by a presumption that becomes the standard?

Social practices are developed from a variety of influences. The challenge to all of us is either (as the impetus in developing the practice or as a follower of the practice) to think about the purpose of the practice. Will it do what it is intended to do; will it be applied equally without discrimination; and will there be procedures in place to prevent abuses. I haven't been good at thinking about some of the social practices I have experienced. Will you be better?

CHAPTER 8 – ANCHORS

We all need an anchor in our lives to provide stability and to make it possible for us to reach out and participate in activities beyond our comfort zones. We have many social supports during our lives and generally, we have several at the same time – family, teachers, church, sports, hobbies, etc. Is there one support that we have during various stages of our lives that is more significant– an anchor? I think so. I believe we sometimes get lost on our journeys through life -- when we lose our anchors. Perhaps multiple or competing commitments, introspection, and major events such as relocation, are the culprits.

We know that social supports are important to all of us, and the lack of them affects our actions. Having someone who will listen to you is important to our well-being and perhaps the lack of a listener is sometimes a contributor to what is an unacceptable behavior. We know that a child being bad to gain attention is evidence that attention, whether positive or negative, is sought. Perhaps this is an illustration of the relationship between social supports and anchors. In this case, the child was searching for more from his social support – his parents. Was this support (or lack of it) an anchor for the child? As a child, I felt strong support from my parents, and they were my primary social support. But were they my anchor? I have always loved to play (and exercise has been play in my mind). I ask myself was exercise my anchor when I was younger or has my anchor always been my family. Perhaps I have always had two anchors with exercise and family being the stabilizing anchors, but I have also always sought change. When my current circumstances become too comfortable, I look for new challenges. In the process, I try to retain my old social supports – family, exercise, and former work and community colleagues. But retaining social supports may be easier for me than it is for others because I am quite happy working at keeping up with these contacts. Others may not have the time or may be so overwhelmed in a new environment that it is not possible. Perhaps the gypsy in me is part of the reason. I like changes and want to continue to grow, do, meet new people, and be.

Many people have faith or religion as a stabilizing anchor throughout their lives. For me, a belief in God has been a constant, but it has not had the same influence on me that I see in others. I don't think I have fully committed to relying on my spiritual commitment as an anchor. Some would argue that this shows a lack of religious commitment. Maybe they are right.

It seems to me that as a society, we are searching for a sense of belonging or of being a part of something. If we look at televised dramas and crisis – Princess Diana's death, airplane crashes, and terrorist bombing -- we see that many people identify with them and take them into their everyday thoughts. Perhaps a feeling of local community and family that was once part of most everyone's life is no longer there for many of us because of our increasing mobility and changing job culture. As a result, this sense of belonging and community is not there to help us in developing our social supports. How many people share common concerns and socialize with their neighbors? Do we hang out with them? Do our children play together? Or do they all go to different schools? Is there a neighborhood gang of children who play together or just gangs? Perhaps it's more difficult today to be part of the local communities in which we live. Technology enables us to be a part of larger groups, and perhaps the smaller community supports are replaced by Facebook, Twitter, Instagram, and texting. If this is true, then it seems more important for us to find what can be our stabilizing anchors, whatever they may be.

I believe that laughing can be a social support and even an anchor for some of us. Laughing is not just for children. Think about what makes you laugh. Most often, I laugh at myself or with someone else when they laugh at themselves. I do and say some stupid things, but I don't always see the humor until after the fact. Case in point -- pulling into a parking space with Jake (who was in the puberty black hole at the time) when the young man in the truck beside me was frustrated with my driving and yelled, "Where'd you get your license, Sears Roebuck?" Wanting to put the young man in his place, I responded quickly but with words that I laugh at every time I think of them. "You ain't got no good manners!" This is so far from what would typically come from my mouth; it puts me in my place and makes me laugh at the same time.

Mother used to giggle every time she scared or startled someone. Phyllis, my sister, used to giggle every time she told a secret, which was always. Sharon, my sister, makes us all smile with her big eyes and naiveté -- when inserting her money card in a machine in Florida (she wasn't sure it was going to work), she turned to us with amazement and said, "It knows me. It said hello Sharon Entry!" Shelly, my daughter, is always laughing at something, often herself, but it makes you want to be around her because laughing is catching.

In trying to think when I laughed hysterically last, nothing comes quickly to mind so I must be taking myself too seriously, and I should stop. Listen to children -- Kaitlin (granddaughter) in a typical day. She is always laughing and giggling. Then listen to yourself in a typical day. How many times did you giggle?

There are many influences on what we embrace as anchors. Many of our anchors are just the most influential social supports. We may lose social supports at various times in our lives, but it is important to know yourself well enough to know when this happens and take steps to either find a new anchor or reacquaint yourself with an old anchor. My sister and I went to a summer camp when we were younger, and we learned to call out to others in the woods if we had lost our way. I'd like to share this call with you. I still call her sometimes and say this chat. She knows what it means about me – I've gotten lost again.

"Hi, lo, enemeanie ca ca, umcha cha and a pee wa wa!"

CHAPTER 9 – PHILOSOPHY

Wiser men and women and those with an intellectual discipline will perhaps view my thinking as illogical, but what is logic but a label defined and described by man. Each man and woman has thoughts, and how can thoughts be right or wrong? Thoughts are. This discussion is not intended to be a debate (which I'm not particularly good at either), but a pathway to stimulate thinking.

One definition found in [12]Merriam-Webster for philosopher "...is a person who seeks wisdom or enlightenment?" One could argue that we are all philosophers to some degree then. The extent to which we pursue enlightenment, how we pursue wisdom, and whether we share the results of our pursuits are what distinguishes us.

Maybe our thoughts don't mature or grow up -- just our verbal and written communications skills. Perhaps this is why so many of us say we don't feel our ages and suggest we still feel as we did when we were 20 or another earlier age. Think back or try to recall your thoughts when you were a child. Were they any different or was only the subject different because of your environmental and educational influences at the time? Can you think in any form other than words? Perhaps this is why we cannot remember things before we could communicate and why we cannot bridge

---

[12] "philosopher." *Merriam-Webster.com.* 2015. http://www.merriam-webster.com, March 17, 2015.

the gap to our subconscious and unconscious feelings. What is the intended use for the rest of our brains? Do all creatures communicate with symbols? But we humans are limited by verbal and written communications? Admittedly, we understand body language, but we interpret the actions with words. How do other animals interpret their body language symbols -- with actions? How do our pets interpret our body language symbols? Did we miss or forget this understanding in our evolutionary process? How do we get it back? Can you think in any other way besides words?

Are lofty principles and thoughts devoid of joy and laughter? I don't know, but my philosophy of life would be misunderstood if I fail to communicate the joy I feel every time I look outside. Outside is wonderful. The sky, the trees, the sun, the moon, the rain, the snow, and even the storms are wonders that I cannot even begin to comprehend, but I can enjoy being in their presence.

The joy of observing a young anything cannot be overstated. Spring is my favorite season for this reason -- buds on the trees, new plant life, baby animals, and baby humans (although not limited to the Spring). The excitement the new ones feel on being, and the playful and joyful way they approach things is a joy that is seldom matched.

What happiness I feel when I perceive that I am an animal that is part of the universe. I cannot imagine the universe's intricacies. I cannot comprehend its physical interrelated design. I cannot perceive its place in the greatness of being, but I feel privileged and great joy at being a part of it. I feel privileged to have been planted where I was and to have the environmental and educational opportunities I've had. This makes me even more appreciative of the life I've been given. To waste it on sadness and sorrow would be a severe misuse.

Philosophy is often spoken about in relation to religion. Or, perhaps religion is often discussed within the context of our philosophy -- our beliefs. And as I age, I understand why so many people search to find the answer to life or perhaps more accurately, the answer to what happens after life. The mass suicide by a religious group is one action that one group took, perhaps in relying on a belief about what happens after death or it may have been the result of just following a very persuasive leader. The most atrocious example of seeking a new path to preserve the life of a particular group of people was Hitler's plan to develop a perfect race. These are extreme examples, but most of us search quietly within ourselves. Years ago, there was a television special and book describing a young man's quest to live a meaningful life. He rid himself of all material wealth and went to Alaska to live off the land. Although he died at a very young age because he mistakenly ate the poisonous part of a plant, his journal left his philosophy of life -- he felt he had lived in his 20 some years more than most people do after three times that number.

Although material possessions have never been important to me, I sometimes find myself coveting certain perceptions people have of me because they seem to symbolize success in other people's eyes. I am not always comfortable enough with my own view of the worth of me to discount completely how other people see me. For example, it's easy for me to live simply in a house or home, but it's not as easy for me to be associated or known as only having achieved work at certain job levels. If the level of the job is below what I have achieved, I find myself wanting to make sure people know I've gone beyond that level. Although in theory, I do not believe the job defines the person; in practicality, I guess I want to make sure it doesn't. Jobs and careers are what we do, but for most of us, it does not define our beliefs, our values, our commitment or lack of commitment to our families, to society, or to ourselves.

Some discuss philosophy within the context of who controls our actions -- God, fate, us, or some combination. Do we have and exercise free will? Is it our ability to make socially acceptable choices? Or, are our moods chemically influenced by the balance or imbalance of hormones in our bodies, making "good" choices more likely on some days and "bad" choices more predominant on others? How free is our will? Is the extent determined by the richness of our environments? If a person lives his or her life as a hermit, without social interactions, does that person have a free will, or are all choices tied to survival?

What is the difference between free will and our conscious? I've always wanted to be a "good person" because it makes me feel badly to be bad and to be thought of poorly by others. Why? Because I was taught, "it's a good thing" as my daughter Jo always says. On the other hand, I can behave in a good way but still have bad thoughts. I may graciously wish someone well who has achieved something great or has a fantastic opportunity, but my inner thoughts may be ones of envy or jealousy. Do we all really want to win? Try as I might I can't always make myself think good thoughts. My Aunt Pearl could. She is one of the special people I was fortunate to know who always had genuine kind thoughts for everyone. I always wanted to be like her, but somehow her constant kindheartedness was in conflict with the competitive me who wanted to be thought of as a hero.

Are our conscious and free will merely another term for thoughts? Are there more than genetic, physical, and environmental influences that define us? If so, how do we know? How do you describe it? Or, perhaps, there's much of the world, of the universe, of ourselves, that we cannot comprehend. Try as we might to find logical explanations, based upon current scientific data, I don't think we can. Isn't it interesting how sure we are of scientific facts and defend them against all challenges, but haven't we seen historically how easily today's fact can be tomorrow's myth? The earth is flat. Eat more protein. Take estrogen only. The polite way to describe these changes I think is, updated information, but this phrase also suggests facts can change or evolve as we learn more. Perhaps in another century or two, we will consider today's medical practices of surgery barbaric -- like cutting off a chicken's head. Going to the moon used to be science fiction. Preserving the physical body in a healthy or perhaps a future state is an area that creates controversy. Cloning is a procedure discussed by some, but it is feared by most because of that "x" dimension of defining our individuality -- soul, consciousness, free will. Whatever you call it, society seems determined not to interfere with it even though we don't understand it and can't agree upon where it comes from. So it seems that each of us has a choice. We can try to nurture that inner soul by being all that we can be, for ourselves and for the universe in which we live. Or, we can ignore the soul and live superficially, like a visitor in the universe, rather than a participant. Which do you choose?

CHAPTER 10 – BEING ALIVE

We are all dying. But are we all living? Some of us are so frightened by the thought of dying that we are afraid to live. Others don't think about death and don't accept it as a reality. Perhaps one of the reasons is that our inner soul and our physical bodies seem to go through life on different tracks. The inner soul may remain a constant and not feel the effects of aging that the physical body does. It's hard to describe what age the inner self -- our soul -- feels or even when we began to realize that there is more to us than our physical and mental faculties. Perhaps it's different for different people. I believe we begin to recognize our souls when we begin to dream -- of winning a prize, of going to college, of getting married, of having children, of being a millionaire, of being President ... of being a hero. At least for me, I think that is when it began for me, and I still feel like that person.

We still have dreams. Society understands dreams of the future for the young, but finds it difficult to imagine that older people have dreams too. However, my soul doesn't want to stop being just because the body is getting tired. I want to wear that body like a favorite pair of jeans -- worn, faded, torn, comfortable, but still going places. Maybe the places I'm going have to be a little different, but I still want to go! The inner me – my soul has not changed. It's hiding in that older body. Nevertheless, it's still there, and resents having both parts treated equally by society. We live longer now, but we live differently as well. Let's continue to be, as we get older -- no matter what circumstances or physical conditions we may encounter. We need to reconcile ourselves to the body wearing out, but let the soul within continue to burn as long as it can.

Health

The failures of the body or mind make us realize that we are not going to live forever. We're confused about which ailments we should accept as normal aging and which ailments should send us scurrying to the doctor. How do we know? The advances in medical technology make treatment for many conditions possible, but are those treatments necessary? How do we know? If you want to ignore ailments and consider them normal aging, are you being foolish or afraid to go to doctors because they might find something. And if you are maturing, the likelihood that you have some condition is great. How do we know? As a society, we have elevated health care as one of the most important issues from both a political and economic standpoint. Moreover, new technology and research focus on cutting edge treatments that give hope to diseases and conditions that have been death sentences in the past. So no wonder it is difficult to put healthcare in perspective on a personal level in a manner that supports our goals for living and our expectations about dying. What will help us make the best healthcare decisions we can for us personally – more education, more input from our families, more faith, more thoughtfulness … What do you think?

Role

We will have many roles throughout our lives. Some will be temporary and some will be constant, but are these roles who we are? My children call me "Helen." And I like this. Helen is who I am. One of my constant roles is "mother," but that is not all that I am. I have many roles – professional, Gerontologist, divorcee, coach, runner, and more. But I am "Helen," and I'm glad my children know the entire me – "Helen," and not just "mother." Some find it disrespectful for my children to call me by my name, rather than

"Mother." I view it as a compliment that shows they really understand who I am.

When I was younger, I believed in my abilities and myself. As we age, our abilities are questioned, probably because of loss of roles that we felt defined whom we were. When others begin to discount our abilities, we begin to see ourselves as less capable as well and thus begin to behave accordingly. The "looking glass" view of self may be more predominant in older people because we have fewer roles to define ourselves as we age. Or, it could be society continues to place more importance on those roles that are paid or that provide a service, and the elderly, if they do work, generally work in jobs that are voluntary, lower paying, or which carry less prestige than those they held when they were younger. As a result, elders are not always viewed as contributing members of the community, of the business world, or even of the family unit. People are expected to retire sometime between 55 and 75 years. Business accepts older men longer to some extent, but usually only at the higher levels. At the lower levels where most of us are, many businesses would prefer to offer the younger employee the employment opportunity. In addition, the family unit is less likely to be an extended family. Families often don't live in the same town or even the same state, and where in the past, many of the social activities were focused around family, now the distance and interests often preclude it, even if desired.

Yet, there is one area where elders are often accepted -- in our political system of elected and appointed officials. Our congressional representatives and even our judges can be older -- often over the traditional retirement age that is practiced by the rest of society. Although this group is composed mostly of men, perhaps this is because women haven't had time to evolve into these positions. I don't know.

We need to look at older people for who they really are, not for the role in which we put them. It's up to all of us – young and old – to recognize that we are a combination of many roles and values, and not just what the physical body or chronological age would suggest.

Value

Growing up, I was taught to respect my elders and that older people had achieved a certain level of wisdom. As I matured, I realized age did not necessarily equate to wisdom, and I was not alone in this realization. Perhaps this new social understanding contributed to a growing negative image of age by some. If people were not wiser as they age and their physical appearance was not attractive, and they no longer held positions of prestige, what was their value? It seems to be a mystery for some. Older people have higher medical costs and present long-term care problems for their families and society. Many older people appear frustrated or even angry at times. Some have declines in their mental capabilities because of disease, and most have one or more chronic physical conditions. I have six. Are older people a value or liability?

I believe more people are beginning to attribute a more positive value to older people, and the challenge is for us to broaden that view by sharing some of the understanding gained through experience and interactions between the age groups. Older adults can provide oral histories of the past and tell us how technology evolved during their lives. They can share struggles they faced. They can share stories of successes and failures. They can listen. They can be our friends. They can contribute to society in very positive ways if we just let them. They do not need to be segregated so they can pursue recreational activities with each other. They have more to offer, still to be, and should remain integrated into society. With an integrated society of young and old people, we can find solutions to scarce medical resources and educate each other about appropriate uses for medical technology, but we need to do it together. Segregation creates tensions. Integration promotes common goals and understanding. We value old people for who they were. We value young people for who they will become -- thus the only period in life that is valued in the present is the middle. Why do we not value the child for how he or she is at the time? Why always talk about "potential?" We love the innocence of children but easily accept that this innocence will not persist. We have expectations for growing up and reaching that sought-after middle period, but children are people too. We should appreciate them and respect them for who they are as children. We should teach them they have value and not to be "seen and not heard."

Old age is a bit more difficult because few seem to value who they are -- not those of us who are old, not those in the middle, and not the children. Seeing elder people in dependent, often condescending relationships with their families may be a contributor to this view. Older people can continue to be contributing members of society even though they are old. Can we continue to move together in the direction of valuing all age categories – young, middle, and old – in the present? I hope so.

Aging

As we age, some of us spend thousands of dollars making changes to our bodies to prevent the wear and tear from aging showing, but the vast majority of society, the ordinary people, can't afford it. We spend lots of time eating right, exercising, and trying not to worry; and this is supposed to slow the deterioration of our bodies as well as help our mental capacities. The reality is, however, that the aging process is a natural part of the life cycle, and our bodies are eventually going to look weathered and worn. But who's inside? The soul inside is the same one that's been inside the whole time.

Many of us practice age denial daily. How many young people argue with someone who charges them less than a posted price? How many older women argue, question, or are offended if a senior citizen discount is offered? I have. We try our best not to be put in the role of senior citizen that other people seem to assume defines us. For us, though, it's those other people who are old, not us.

Death

Before medical technology enabled us to keep people alive in various states of less than a functioning capacity, most elderly people "lived until they died." This isn't true today. If we loosely define living as a contributing member of society, many of us will live beyond this stage. My Grandpa and Aunt Mame (his common-low wife) both died in their sleep. Aunt Mame just didn't wake up one morning. Grandpa had tuberculoses and although no longer infected, he lived by himself in a rooming house where a few other older men lived, and that is where he died. This was not true for my Mother and Father. Both died in the hospital after considerable suffering. Neither had been consciously communicating for some time before they died. Their deaths were infinitely more difficult for their families, and I have to think, for them as well. What did medical technology give us -- loss of our ability to see our elders as who they really are or at least contribute to it; a more difficult parting for family members, financial burdens for families and the elder person, endless paperwork, and a more frightening death for all. Many have written about death and dignity, and many believe that death with dignity can only be achieved by a few lucky ones. Hospitals, nursing homes, continuing care facilities, are often places where people go to wait to die -- not to live until they die.

I recently heard a reference in a television commercial that is germane to this "waiting period." The essence of the commercial was, "what are all of the baby boomers going to do with the rest of their lives." To me, this implies, the valued part of their lives is over and now comes the filler. In my view, we need to learn how to extend the value part and eliminate the filler. To do this, those of us who start in the filler period must refuse to enter. Fight, scream, cry -- do anything but stay in the value period. If a few of us remain, others will follow, and the value period will gradually come to encompass older ages. Let's don't accept medical technology as the only answer. If it can't keep us from dying, and if there is no hope for returning to living, do we need to choose it?

Some people facing death in a short-term say that once the realization and acceptance of death is made, living becomes better. When I think of going to sleep each night and giving up that inner me, I realize I do it without fear because I know I will be back again in a few hours. How often have we been in such pain that all we want to do is go to sleep and give that inner person (soul) a rest from the pain? Perhaps this is how people who are in chronic pain feel who seek death as a release.

But it seems such a waste to give up a life until you just have to. I believe in the struggle. People of faith believe they will exist after death if they live their lives consistent with the principles and practices of their faith. My belief is somewhat different. I believe in a supreme being, but I cannot begin to comprehend the plan or structure of the universe. I believe life is a privilege no matter what form -- animal, plant, fish, or human. I believe the life force that returns to earth lives on but whether my inner soul will exist after I die, I don't know. But whether I'll care after I die, how could I? It's the anticipation of giving it up that I hate, but I know we all have to and that we are all alone in that process. Death cannot be avoided, and it shouldn't be shunned as an inappropriate topic. It is a reality that we cannot change so worrying about it can only adversely affect the quality of living. Perhaps if we quit trying to avoid facing and discussing death, we can come to accept it as a natural part of life.

I find it difficult to understand how anyone can not believe in something superior to us when you try to comprehend the human body, the earth, the universe ... I don't believe death will be bad, but I have no idea what it will be for our conscious selves. It may be something even more wonderful than we could possibly imagine, or it may be the end of our current consciousness. We can't remember how we felt when we first had life, regardless of when you believe this takes place. The newborn baby was happy, I think, in her mother's womb, and is frightened when first being introduced to the outside world. Life outside the womb to a newborn may be feared by the newborn in a way similar to how death is feared by the living, but newborns come to realize that life is a good thing and don't remember their state of being prior to the introduction to life outside the womb. Perhaps in death, we don't remember life before death but come to recognize our new state of being as equally wonderful. I don't know, but we'll all find out. Death is like having a baby. You can't control when it will come, and you don't know how much it will hurt. But if the result is half as wonderful as a new life, what a wonderful experience death will be.

Living

One definition of living that I found defines living as [13]"the condition of being alive." That almost makes it sound like an ailment, and perhaps it is. But if it is, I think it is a very good ailment! Many people have written about the joy of living, and depending upon our individual circumstances at that particular moment, we may or may not agree that life is a joy. We are not all planted or grown in places that give us the same opportunities, the same privileges, the same obstacles, or the same prejudices, but we all have a unique ability of self. Some may argue, and convincingly that we make our own opportunities, and I tend to agree to a point. The inner soul has a great ability to be, regardless of the circumstances in which we are placed and can struggle and reach for new mountaintops and new opportunities with uncanny ability. The kinds of struggles and opportunities may be dictated by the fields in which we are planted and the nourishment we receive -- educational, emotional, physical, and social. Who is to judge the quality or the importance of the struggles? A child growing up in a cabin on top of a mountain that learns to read, a child who grows up in wealth in Boston who attends Harvard Law School -- whose struggle, whose life is more significant? Whose life is more meaningful?

---

[13] living. (n.d.) *American Heritage® Dictionary of the English Language, Fifth Edition.* (2011). Retrieved March 17 2015 from http://www.thefreedictionary.com/living

The quality of life should not be judged merely by traditional accomplishments of profession or prestige, but by the legacy that life leaves to others. What is more important -- setting an example of behaving with the highest integrity and adherence to honesty and fair play or achieving a position, no matter how it is obtained, of President of a large company? Who will remember and learn from someone becoming President of a company unless the journey (or the struggle) to achieve that position was marked by behavior that demonstrated unusual kindness and thoughtfulness, impeccable integrity in actions, and consistent compassion for people. What if the rise to President is characterized by backstabbing and unscrupulous behavior -- what is the legacy of that accomplishment?

The charismatic leader who makes people want to follow him or her presents another area for discussion. If that leader was able to influence hundreds of people in a very positive way and to inspire them to do good, be good, or be happy, has that leader's life been successful even if the leader did not believe in the talk he presented. Who is to judge the value of life -- others or yourself? Perhaps it's both; I'm not sure. I frequently quote from a James Russell Lowell's poem "…For the gift without the giver is bare." Perhaps the life without the commitment to the struggle is bare as well.

If we only stop and put our lives in perspective with the universe, perhaps we can see the privilege we have in living in it. Watching a male bird give a female bird a worm ... what a rush. Watching the sun come up behind the mountain, watching the waves break over a sandbar ... what a rush. Listening to a young child giggle, listening to a symphony or a lone guitar, listening to a puppy's growl, listening to frogs peep ... what a rush. Observing an older gentleman take his lady's hand, observing planes flying in formation or geese flying in formation, observing a child learning to ride a bicycle or a fawn stand ... what a rush. How exciting life is if we stop to listen and observe. Perhaps we can then begin to see our place in it.

There is one emotion that I believe is the most important one to nurture throughout our lives – love. It is important to have the love we demonstrate for others and the love we receive from others. Some of us focus on the love of a higher power, some, the love of family, and still others the love of a soul mate. Which brings us more joy – the act of receiving love or the act of giving love, or do we have to have both. I don't know. But I'd like to end with a little story about a friend of mine who I believe lived life well. Then you decide the answer.

A Life Well Lived

Floyd grew up in a small town in North Carolina – Rhodhiss, a mill town on the river. Floyd and his family lived in one of the houses provided for the mill workers. He remembers when electricity first came to the small houses. Electricity was turned off and on by a master switch, and the lights all went out at a set time (6:00) p.m. in the evening.

Floyd attended a small Baptist church, and his future wife, Jewel (two years his junior), also attended the same church. Although they attended different schools, they stayed in touch through their church activities. And, one evening after both graduated from high school, Jewel's father saw Floyd kissing Jewel, and Floyd told her father he was going to marry Jewel. Jewel's father just looked at him and said, "I guess that will be all right."

Floyd had three careers -- serving his country, flying and surviving 35 missions as a Bombardier/Navigator on a B17 in World War II, as an executive in the textile industry, and as an owner and broker of a real estate firm. Floyd and Jewel are engaged members of their local community and live active productive lives – adapting to new and changing abilities with grace.

Floyd and Jewel are both in their nineties now, and one day I asked Floyd what was one of the happiest times in his life. Floyd immediately answered, "That would have to be June 28, 1940." I asked why, and he said that was the day he and Jewel were married. Floyd and Jewel recently celebrated their 74th wedding anniversary, and I asked Floyd what was his secret for being married so long. He simply said, "It would have to be my love for Jewel."

Part III -- ME

CHAPTER 11 – BACKGROUND

Life with My Parents

I was born in a small Midwestern town in Indiana. My father worked in one of the many local factories, and my mother was a "housewife." Rather than being referred to as a "stay-at-home" mom as we would refer to her today, she was a "housewife" and wore housedresses – not jeans or slacks. Most women did not work outside the home, but my mother did take in ironings and for a while, worked in a local restaurant.

My mother was married twice and had three children with her first husband – two girls (Phyllis and Betty) and one boy (Joe). I always referred to them as the first litter, but we were all close even though there was a significant age

This is my grandmother in a housedress similar to the type my mother would have worn.

difference. As is true for most of us, as we grow older, age differences seem to become less of a difference. My mother married my father one Christmas eve; I believe the ceremony took place in the house we lived in; but I'm not sure. My father and mother had two children – my sister, Sharon, who is two years my senior, and me. My father's mother died in childbirth, and his mother's sister, Aunt Mame, moved in with them to take care of my dad, his brother and sister.

I was named after my father's sister, my Aunt Helen. Aunt Helen was a successful professional, working for the Los Angeles Times. This was significant for the time in which she lived when fewer women pursued careers. Her husband was a stay-at-home husband, and they were both comfortable and happy with this relationship – again ahead of their times. They had an apartment in the  city and a house in Sherman Oaks with a pool and a beautiful and well-kept patio. I don't know why my father named me after her, but I loved it, especially the added attention and gifts she gave me.

One of the things I find interesting now is that I called my Mother, mother, and my father, Dad or Daddy. My sister Sharon called Mother, Momma, and I don't remember what she called our Dad. Perhaps she was more of a Momma's girl, and I was more of a Daddy's girl … ummm

I often think of myself as being very much like the Mother Goose rhyme,

> "There was a little girl,
>
> Who had a little curl,
>
> Right in the middle of her forehead.
>
> And when she was good,
>
> She was very, very good,
>
> But when she was bad, she was horrid!"

Source: The Real Mother Goose (1916)

You may agree after you read further

CHAPTER 12 – FAMILY

My family, both immediate and extended, is vastly important to me and is my first priority. I have always felt the responsibility to be there for all of my family and to nurture the family support network. I am one of the persistent organizers of family reunions. My sister, Phyllis, hosted the first family reunion, and perhaps she was the one who taught me to be a fierce supporter of family. You could always rely on her to support you, no matter what. When my former and estranged husband's father died, I was several states away and could not attend the funeral services, so Phyllis went to the memorial service for me but made it clear that she was there for me.

My parents taught me to play by example. As a young girl, we often went to Grandpa and Aunt Mame's house or they came to ours, and we played poker. On the weekends, we went on picnics. Mother always made fried chicken, potato salad, deviled eggs, and chocolate cake. I wish I could eat this meal just one more time! Daddy played golf or fished, and we were allowed to fish with him, if it was a fishing weekend. Mother sometimes rode on the merry-go-round with us, laughing the whole time, and if my Dad was around, he joined in by pushing us all.

When I was in elementary school, I had a pocketknife that I played a game called Mumbley Peg with my friends. We sat outside in the grass and played for hours, throwing the knife through a series of pre-defined movements. (I think this was a variation from the original game.) I don't remember for sure, but I think my Dad taught me how to play. Now having a pocketknife would be seen as dangerous and irresponsible by parents. Back then, it wasn't. In addition, I had a homemade bow that my brother-in-law, Lane, made for me. I was the "tomboy" in the family and always eager to play whatever game was being played. There was a vacant lot next to one of my friend's house, and it was our gathering place. We played softball,  football, and kick ball. The people who owned the lot didn't seem to mind that we thought of the lot as our own special playground.

I remember our house as being "easy to be in." My friends always wanted to be at our house, and Mother frequently fed more than just her own family. Even though we didn't have much, everyone was always welcome. She was a good cook; she could make something wonderful out of nothing. One of my friends loved her "homgoo," and one day Mother accidently dropped most of the box of salt into the homgoo. She was ready to throw it away, but my friend loved it so much that she took it home and ate it anyway. One of the things Mother loved to do when my friends spent the night at our house was to scare us. She would sneak outside and knock on the window. And when we screamed, she laughed so hard that she wet her pants.

When my sister and I were growing up, I was the responsible one in the family. One time when my mother and dad were in LA visiting my Aunt, my sisters, Phyllis and Sharon were both at home when our dog, Stormy, threw up in the kitchen. It sat there all day until I came home much later in the day. They knew I would clean it up. Although they were right, I did clean it up I still berated them the whole time. But it didn't matter. They knew I would always take care of what needed to be done.

Sharon, my sister, and I went to what was the only high school in our town at the time. Now I believe there are about three. Although Sharon and I fought frequently over bobby pins and had very different interests, we still supported each other in the activities that were important to us. Sharon was the actor in the family, and I still refer to her as my sister, the actor. She was President of the Thespian Society and was usually the lead actor in school plays. It was customary to send telegrams (we still had local telegrams then) to wish the actors well before a play. I always sent one to "Pieface," which is what I called her and signed it "Fliptop," which is what she called me. I don't remember now where those names came from, but we still use those names today. I was into cheerleading, and I remember trying out for cheerleading when I was a freshman. I was very nervous and when I went up to the stage, I stayed on the side of the stage and didn't get close to the middle where I should have been. But I also remember looking out at the audience, and seeing my sister Sharon there. She always was. I later made cub cheerleading but never made varsity, which was a disappointment to me. I also made Dramatic Club and Thespian Society, but I probably had an inside track because of my sister. I was never good at acting. I was better at being a student-director.

<u>Christmas</u>

To me, family and Christmas go together, and Christmas is my favorite time of the year. When it was just Sharon and I at home with Mother and Dad, Christmas time was quiet but special. One of our favorite things to do was to drive around the neighborhoods and look at all the Christmas lights on the houses. Back then, people spent a lot of time decorating their houses. When it got close to Christmas, my Dad would take us to the Christmas tree lot to pick out our tree. He always tried to make us wait until a week before Christmas, but we pestered him until sometimes he would give in and take us a few days earlier. We brought the tree home with its wood stand nailed on the bottom and put it in front of our picture window so we could admire it from the outside as well as from the inside. I don't remember watering the tree so we must not have had tree stands then, which is probably why we didn't get a tree until a week before Christmas. On Christmas Eve, Daddy would make what he called seafoam, and Mother would make chocolate fudge. Then we would sit around the tree and sometimes watch a Christmas show on TV or just eat and talk.

As a little girl, I loved giving Christmas presents to everyone, but I didn't have any money until I received a card from my Aunt Helen, which contained a check -- her Christmas present to me. Then I would go downtown and buy Blue Waltz perfume (I think it was 15 cents a bottle) for all the women and white handkerchiefs (10 cents each) for all the men. I didn't realize at the time that doing this gave me more joy than those receiving the gifts.

I kept my love for Christmas as a young adult and started a tradition with my children of going to a Christmas tree farm to select and cut down our Christmas tree. We went to the same farm for years while the children were growing up. The farm was located in the mountains, and we rode or walked behind a wagon to take our Christmas tree back  to the farm entrance. There, we had help tying the tree on the top of our car. It was a familiar experience when we returned every year because the same family continued to own and operate the Christmas tree farm. We spent hours on the farm, selecting just the right tree, but sometimes the girls would trick Jake because he just couldn't decide which tree to pick. They would bring him back

to a tree he had looked at earlier and sort of liked and make him think he was seeing it for the first time as the "perfect" tree.

If we were lucky, it snowed while we were there, and we had snowball fights and made snow angels. Afterwards, we always stopped in Front Royal to have

sandwiches at a local fast food place. Often some of my children's friends or even parents of their friends came with us.

I still love having a live tree, but I think I'm probably the only one as I see this tradition disappearing. My children placate me by letting me have a live tree (even though we rarely cut one down anymore), but I think having a live tree has lost the magic it once had for them, even though it hasn't lost it for me.

I usually make butter cookies for Christmas for everyone to decorate, and in the past, we had cookie decorating contests that everyone took very

seriously. Also, I set up a crafts table during the Christmas season so everyone could make decorations for the tree. Shelly has adopted the craft-making tradition, and she stocks all sorts of materials to make decorations. I think this tradition will continue, but I think the cookie decorating contest may be about to disappear. Perhaps making

Christmas stockings for everyone (plus a couple for guests) will replace it. The girls and I (Shelly and me are usually the instigators) have made at least three sets of Christmas stockings in recent years. And the last time we made stockings, we even made Christmas hats.

I used to make little gift packages of cookies, candy and banana bread for friends and neighbors. After Becky moved away, she often came to my house so we could make our gift packages together. It took a long time because we both had many people on our lists. After we quit making the gifts for our neighbors, we still got together occasionally to make fudge and divinity. It was a happy time because we laughed a lot when the divinity splattered everywhere!

When the children all lived at home, I had open house Christmas Eve. I cooked and baked for the weeks before Christmas and invited everyone to come Christmas Eve for food and fun. We usually played Charades at least some time during the evening. I also made gifts for everyone, even my children's friends. I was often caught finishing a gift for my children's friends when they came to our house on Christmas Eve. As everyone grew older and moved away from home, Christmas has evolved into our spending the whole week before Christmas together, at the beach in the Outer Banks, my house in Clarksville, or Fripp Island. I think I like this even better because we have the whole week of uninterrupted fun.

Married Life

I was married shortly before my 20th birthday. Right after the ceremony, my husband and I moved to Bloomington, Indiana so my husband could attend Indiana University. I had a job working full time in the Motion Picture Production Department, and he worked part-time for a local Pediatrician. Herman Wells was the Chancellor of the University at the time, and he and his mother attended the same church we did. One morning, they were sitting right behind us, and Chancellor Well's Mother said, "Hermie, these are some of your students," and started a conversation with us. They were both very unassuming and personable.

We lived in a 29-foot trailer, which could be challenging at times. The bedroom was the bed! The pipes froze often, and I remember waking up with frost on the inside of the windows. And we were poor, but our friends who were students too were poor also so we didn't mind so much. We went to movies occasionally, and often we pooled our food with our neighbors for group meals. Everything was shared – beer, relatives when they brought goodies, and any kind of food that was a treat.

Our first child was born while we lived in the trailer, but my husband had just joined the State Police and was in training so he could not be there when our baby girl, Jo, was born. Our good friends and neighbors took me to the hospital, and all the neighbors in our student trailer park, took turns visiting me in the hospital. I think it was normal to stay in the hospital a couple of days at that time. When I came home from the hospital with a new baby, my Mother came down for a week to help me. After that, I was alone. I was scared, and it took me a while to get the hang of it. I timed how long I would allow my baby to cry (at the Pediatrician's suggestion), but I think I couldn't manage more than five minutes. After I got the hang of it, I was probably over protective and didn't want anyone to disrupt her schedule. I now thought I knew everything.

I didn't want to go back to work and leave my baby girl even though I liked working at the Motion Picture Production Department at the University. I set up the department to catalog and mail films, learned to type storyboards, and learned about animation. It was interesting, and I liked the people. When the head of the department received his PhD, the staff painted his office door in various colors and patterns, and he came to see me in our trailer after Jo was born. He offered to let me have as much time as I needed, but by that time, my husband had finished his training, and had an assignment in central Indiana.

So it was not long after Jo was born that we moved to a small town in central Indiana where our second child, Shelly, was born. The hospital sent Shelly home in a large red Christmas stocking. Shelly was born on December

23, but I had to cry to the doctor, so I could come home on Christmas day. I was animate about wanting to come home since I had another child at home, waiting for Santa to come. This childbirth experience was much easier because I knew what to expect, and I was not alone during the first several months as I had been when Jo was born. My Mother-in-Law came to help me right after I came home from the hospital with Shelly, but it ended up being more work for me because she was very careful not to step on my toes. And I was probably overly assertive and confident in my abilities, which made it difficult for her. I was more confident in my mothering and homemaker abilities then and had time to look for other things to stimulate my thinking. I was typing for a client in my home and for a local Justice of the Peace in one of the surrounding communities.

My third child, Becky, was born in this same small town, but by this time, we had moved to the first house that we could purchase. It was new construction, and we had a loan that enabled us to do some of the finishing work as part of our down payment. We painted the entire inside and finished all the yard work – rotor tilling and seeding. The house was in a neighborhood where we had an opportunity to make friends and socialize with our neighbors. Many are still my good friends even though I don't go back to Indiana that frequently.

Dr. Bill, delivered Becky, but basically, he just "caught her." He was the stereotypical country doctor. He called you if you were sick; made house calls; and if he thought you were really sick, he would say, "Oh my God, you need to see a doctor!" and refer you appropriately. But his nurse Evelyn ran a tight ship, and most of us were a little afraid of her. She left pills in the waiting room with our names on them, and we didn't ask any questions – just did what we were told. Dr. Bill's wife, Julie, called us if she thought your doctor bills were getting too high. She didn't want you to have to pay too much. Later I taught Julie to swim when I was teaching swimming at the high school. It was a fun class that I still remember fondly. Everyone in the class was engaged and supportive, and most of all, they all had fun – including me.

Shortly after Becky was born, the neighborhood children kept coming to the door to see the new baby. I couldn't figure out why there was so much interest until I caught my other two children, Jo and Shelly, collecting a dime from these visitors as an admission price to see the baby! I have many happy memories from living in this neighborhood. In fact, one of my good neighborhood friends, Shirley, had my daughter, Shelly, convinced that her last name was theirs, Oeffinger. She thought her name was Oeffinger until she went to kindergarten.

During this time, I was coaching a swim team during the summer and teaching swimming at the local high school. When I was given the opportunity to coach the swim team, I went back to my hometown to visit the coaches for the YMCA swim team for which I swam. I remember wearing heels to the pool area to talk to them. I guess I thought it would make me seem more important, but in reality, I think it just showed how much I wanted to impress them. I soon became more confident with my coaching and was my usual bossy self. (I think I have always been a bit bossy and want to control the situation.) I had 60 children on the swim team ranging in age from five to 17, and they wouldn't throw me in the water (as was customary after winning a meet) unless they asked me first. I coached the team for several years and put on an annual water show with intricate synchronized swimming routines, announcers, clowns, and printed programs. I was fortunate to gain participation by a broad group of family volunteers. We had a sound system, lighting, bleachers, props to use in the routines in the water, and costumes designed by a designer at a local fabric factory. I tend to broaden whatever task I am given, and this was true even with the water show. This is both good and bad but a characteristic that I continue to exhibit.

My fourth child was born when we lived in this neighborhood. Another of my neighborhood friends, Betty, was a nurse, and she was in the delivery room with me. This was before husbands were encouraged to share in the delivery process. By this time, I had started back to college in Indianapolis, and Jake, my son, was born over Spring break. I took my books to the hospital with me. (I had all my children by natural childbirth.) When I came home from the hospital, the three girls all had chicken pox, and I think one or two had pinworms – all in the life of a mother!

We only stayed in this house for about a year after Jake was born. My husband and I had started having trouble, and although I suspected he was seeing someone else, I hadn't confronted him. Nevertheless, we moved to an old house in town and spent some time fixing it up. I took the kids to the park and played tennis with the local tennis group. We didn't have to arrange to play tennis with anyone. We just went to the park, and we all took turns playing. In fact, those who weren't playing watched Jake in his portable crib. An older woman, named Helen, taught most of us to play tennis, but she taught us more than playing tennis. She taught us to be good sports and to have fun while playing. She always had a smile on her face, and every spring, she painted her garage door with red polka dots. Later I had Helen in a swimming class. Because she was so muscular, thin but muscular, she sank easily – but always with a smile on her face.

During this time, I was still going to school, but my married life, fell apart. And it was not pretty. I survived though, got a full-time job in Indianapolis and completed my undergraduate degree. I worked as a secretary for the Director of IT in an insurance company, and he turned out to be a very good boss. He had never had a secretary before so he was flexible. The day before I was supposed to start my new job, I contracted a very bad case of the flu and was in bed for a full week. He was very understanding and let me delay my start date a week. While I was finishing my degree, I left home at 6:00 a.m. and didn't get home until close to midnight. I employed an older woman who lived across the street to come to our house to care for the children, and I was probably not a very good mother during this time since I was tired and had to find some time to study on the weekends. When I resigned this position, my boss had me type my going away present – Desiderata. I had not read it at the time and loved it instantly. People continue to amaze me. I never would have suspected that my boss would find Desiderata and want to share it with me. I have been fortunate throughout my life to meet good people that I always consider my friends.

Shortly after graduation, I was ready to have a fresh start so my sister who lived in Georgia at the time, arranged for me to interview for a job at Fannie Mae in Atlanta. I was hired; sold the house in Indiana; and moved to Atlanta, Georgia to an apartment that I had not seen. My sister lived nearby in Athens, Georgia and picked out the apartment for me. Our furniture at the time consisted of a plastic couch, a card table and chairs, our mattresses and box springs, and a couple of chests. I made $8,000 a year as a Loan Clerk. The children made the adjustment better than I expected, but I remember laying in bed that first night thinking first – "what have I done;" followed by, "I can go anywhere and do anything I want!"

I didn't have a babysitter for Jake, who was only two and one-half at the time; but I lucked out. A family that lived below us in the apartment complex was waiting for their house to be built. They had two young girls, and Arlene, the mother, agreed to watch Jake. She continued to watch him after they moved to their new house, and Jake stayed with her the whole time we lived in Atlanta. I was now on my way to starting my career.

CHAPTER 13 – CAREERS

I received my undergraduate degree in Elementary Education, but because I was now a single mother, I didn't think teaching was the best option for me. I believed, and still believe, that you have to give much of yourself to be a good teacher. I could not give everything I needed to my four children and have enough left to give to be a good teacher, which is why my sister arranged the interview opportunity for me at Fannie Mae in Atlanta.

I was at the bottom of the organizational structure as a Loan Clerk, but I learned as much as I could about the broader organization and tasks associated with the various positions. At times though, I think I was seen as a "know-it-all" by some of my female co-workers, and I was still sometimes treated with less respect by at least one of my clients. It got so when that particular client came into the office; my co-workers knew I saw "red" when he referred to me as "honey," so they alerted me when he entered the reception area. Nonetheless, I was rewarded for my hard work by being promoted every six months during the two years we lived in Atlanta. At the same time, I was learning about being a single mother and balancing that with my career. My former husband quit paying child support about six months after we moved to Atlanta so we had to move to a less expensive apartment. This wasn't all bad because we didn't feel like we were particularly poor, even though we were. I qualified for food stamps but never found it necessary to take advantage of the benefit. We hiked Stone Mountain. The first time I was in my high heels. We found a tree that had a large opening at the bottom that we always crawled through when we were climbing the mountain. Often, when I came home from work, I would meet the kids and jump in the pool with my clothes on. We also learned to camp. I bought a tent and took it in the box along with the kids and the dog to the campground at Stone Mountain. We learned to put the tent up at the park, and I think the kids learned not to be afraid to try new things since

they were active participants in the learning process. My youngest daughter, Becky, became a Bluebird, so I became a Bluebird leader; Jo, my oldest had a gang of friends and even played girls basketball for the girl's team, although typically she sought non-team activities. Jo also saved the money that I paid her for

babysitting her siblings in the summer (after hiring several other unacceptable babysitters) to buy a horse. She had taken a few riding lessons when we lived in Indiana. I, of course, knew nothing about horses, but I took her to look at several horses within her budget. She ultimately found a 12-year old quarter horse that she named Sarge; and because our apartment backed to pastures owned by a local attorney, she contacted him before we went on our search to see if she could keep her horse in his pastures with his other horses. It was worth her effort. He agreed to let her keep a horse on his property if she provided the feed and even told her she could have a stall if she cleaned one out. How lucky is that! But I learned later through my children that this is where the Klan held some meetings, and where my children snuck some of the refreshments they served.

The children were all close during this time and hadn't started the sibling fighting that would take place later when they moved into the black hole of puberty. One day, I had a call at the office from a couple crying girls, I couldn't tell who was hurt or if anyone was hurt since both Jo and Shelly were crying. Apparently, one of the neighbors had tried to discipline Shelly for verbally defending herself against his son. When I got home, I immediately went to this man's house and told him in no uncertain terms that he was never to attempt to discipline any of my children and if he had anything to say, he should contact me!

My work sent me for a weeklong training in Miami to attend Mortgage Banking School. This was a nice reprieve for a single Mom. We stayed in dormitory rooms so I quickly formed a gang of fellow students – both male and female, and we talked the dining room into packing us a lunch so we could go to the beach for a picnic. We played tennis, went to the dog races, played pool and ping pong, and studied together. It was like having the college dorm room experience that I never had.

One of the women who worked for me in the Georgia office said she used to work for Coretta King. She was a young Black woman who always made me laugh, particularly when she told me she was afraid to date one young man because he was so black that he was blue, which scared her.

Now that I was feeling more comfortable in my role as a single working mom, I was ready to take the next step professionally and applied for a job that would be a promotion in the Washington, DC office. I got the job! So, this meant I had to find a place to live and move four children (one still needing a babysitter during the day) and a dog to DC. My relocation expenses were paid for by the company, but the rest of the logistics, including finding care for my children when I had to travel overnight, were all mine. I found a townhouse to rent, found a babysitter to care for Jake half days since he was enrolled in kindergarten the other half days, and found a couple who were seminary students to stay overnight to care for the children when I had to travel. It was a good thing since I was sent on a weeklong out-of-state trip the second week on the job.

I had to earn respect from my new co-workers since I was the new kid from Georgia, especially since I was promoted six months after I arrived. It took a while not to be seen as the person to take notes or get the coffee in meetings because I was a female. It was a male dominated network, and I had to work even harder to gain respect from some of the older men. But I was getting there. I just had to be better at everything I did. And, I had to be creative in making sure that because I was a single female with four children that this didn't prevent me from doing my job just like the men. For example, Jake had not had chickenpox and neither had his babysitter's children so when he got chickenpox after only being in DC for a few months, I had to hire a

sitter full-time from a babysitting service. This was not only scary because I didn't really know anything about the people they would send except for what the agency told me, but it was expensive since I had to employ the agency for a week. Further, when the other children got sick at school, I had to have another child  take the sick child home and stay with her until I got home. It was a team effort with my children and me.

I held several other positions while in D.C. from Assistant Director to Director, and during that time, I was particularly proud of those projects that crossed departmental lines in which I created collaborative teams and made it a good and fun experience for those working on the projects. One of the projects was developing and presenting to the President, one of the first risk analysis.

Another was developing a Lender Report Card system. During the development of the Lender Report Card, I demonstrated the PC to the President, and my colleagues in IT were frightened because usually they wanted to lock me in a room. I saw no boundaries and had the IT Department run 20 or 30 PCs overnight to upload data to the mainframe. We were on the bleeding edge (as my IT colleague referred to what we were doing) of PCs since the largest capacity disk we had then was 60 mg. I always thought we should make work fun, and I had more of an opportunity to do this when I could create projects or teams.

We stayed in that first townhouse that we moved to from Georgia for a year. Our next move was to a house that had four bedrooms in a nice suburb in Northern Virginia. We called this house, "the white house." This meant that all of my children had their own room, and we lived in this house when all three girls were in the black hole of puberty. We rented the house for about six years, and I was grounded most of the time because the girls were. But this is also the house we lived in when my middle daughter, Shelly, was carried out by an intruder when I was not home. Becky, Jake and I were camping in West Virginia, and Jo and Shelly stayed home. When we came home, Jo met me at the door and said Shelly was all right so immediately I knew something bad had happened. Jo explained what had happened. Shelly and one of her friends were upstairs asleep and Jo and her boyfriend Mike were downstairs. The house was on two levels and had two glass sliding doors – one upstairs and one downstairs. The glass sliding doors had not been locked for the night. The intruder came in the upstairs glass sliding door, and Jo and Mike heard screams and immediately ran out the front door and around to the back of the house. The intruder dropped Shelly at the side yard, and Mike continued to chase him. Although he didn't catch him, he came back and helped Shelly breathe in a bag because she was hyperventilating. I still feel like throwing up when I think about how this experience made Shelly feel.

This event involving Shelly, and one that happened to my son Jake, are the two that still make my heart ache. When it happened to Jake, I was not there also. The couple who spent the night while I was out-of-town dropped him off at his daytime sitter but did not wait to see if he got in okay. As it happened, the sitter had an emergency, was not at home, so Jake was outside in the yard crying until a neighbor heard him crying and took him in to take care of him. What made matters worse is that I didn't hear about this until weeks later when the neighbor told me. Neither Jake nor my sitters told me. I felt like a bad mother for both of these incidences since I was not there to protect my children. After Shelly's experience, the children were all afraid and came into my bedroom to sleep so that I finally put all of their mattresses on the floor in my bedroom, and that's where we all slept for about a year. Every time someone heard a noise, I had to get up and investigate. I remember going down the stairs followed by all of the kids with what they had found as a weapon of choice – tennis racquets or baseball bats. We looked for signs of the

intruder in the neighborhood for days. We did routine inspections around the house, put glass on the roof that he had climbed up on to see in, and were in close contact with the local police, who had teams staking out our house by hiding in the woods behind it. We got through it and did not let it keep us from doing the things we wanted to do. We just became more observant.

Fortunately, the intruder and another window peeper who admitted to looking in our windows were both caught a couple of years later. We were a prime target for window peepers it seems, with three high school age girls and all of their friends always at our house.

The time we lived in the white house was not all bad. We camped almost every weekend in the warmer months. We went to Assateague in the summer, to Jekyll Island, Georgia for Spring Break and to Nags Head, North Carolina for Memorial Day and Fourth of July. We played volleyball on the beach, sang songs around the campfire, and hiked. In fact, we hiked the 26 miles of Assateague Island twice! It was always drag Becky and carry Jake while telling them "It's just around the corner!" Jake tried to rescue all the beached horseshoe crabs on one of the hikes. One particular trip to the beach was memorable. Mike, Jo's boyfriend at the time and long-time family friend, and I decided to take a walk along the part of

the ten-mile stretch of the beach that you could not access by car. We were walking along when a nude man came walking toward us. I was very intimidated so told Mike, "Let's turn around." He said, "No, want to see girls." Apparently, we had stumbled onto a nude beach! Since the only way to get to the area was to hike in, they must have felt they were isolated enough from the other beach-goers.

In the winter, we skied and usually skied on New Year's Day because the slopes were not crowded. And throughout the year, we often spent weekends with my sister and her family at either our house or hers, playing cards – Euchre and Spades.

One of the not so good things I learned during this time was to drink with my colleagues at work. But I came to realize that I was losing control and drinking too much, especially when I began to drink alone. I suspected I was an alcoholic so I went to a counselor for help who wanted me to go to a group counseling session, which I found wasn't for me so she sent me to an AA meeting instead. But I didn't know what to wear so I called my sister, Sharon, to ask her. I think I just wore jeans. The first AA meeting I went to alone was an open meeting, but it was the hardest meeting I would ever attend since I had no idea what to expect and what would be expected of me. I subsequently went to other meetings and became more comfortable. I did not have any difficulty in giving up drinking. I was self-conscious about not drinking at first. I thought everyone was looking at me, but I soon found out, no one was. I don't think my drinking caused me a problem at work, but I think it could have if I didn't recognize the problem when I did. In recent years, I have been able to drink moderately without any of my previous excessive tendencies so perhaps I was using alcohol as an escape in my earlier years. I wish I was a moderate, but I don't seem to be in anything I do – I do everything with enthusiasm.

My father became very ill while I worked in DC, and my sister, Sharon, and I flew out immediately when he was admitted to the hospital. I was there probably around ten days – taking turns staying at night with him in the hospital until he died. I was fortunate to have a great boss then because I had not called work at all during this entire time. My boss called one day to see how things were, but it was clear to him that my family came first before anything else. I was lucky because not everyone has that kind of support from his or her supervisors. And, it gave me an example to follow with people I supervise.

I was now making enough money that I could finally buy a house so I found a townhouse that I could afford in the northern Virginia area, and we moved to the townhouse from the white house. By this time, Jo had graduated from high school and attended Virginia Tech; Shelly had graduated and was working part-time; Becky was a senior coming out of the black hole, and Jake was running with me in the mornings and had a paper route. I was running 5 and 10k races and playing quite a bit of tennis.

Shelly and I were avid exercise enthusiasts during this time and were heavy into doing aerobics and working out. We decided to research the possibilities of opening our own aerobics/fitness studio. Although we were both working full-time, we made time to do the research. We attended an aerobics camp in Boston, and I attended training at Nautilus in Florida. I enrolled in an American College of Sports Medicine training course and passed with a certification as an Exercise Leader, and we met with an attorney. But we weren't done with our research so we enlisted my sister, Sharon, to do a cost-flow analysis for us. After doing all of this research, we decided we would not be profitable if we operated the facility in the manner we felt best. At that time, there were a lot of gyms going under, and many did not employ qualified instructors. We could still enjoy exercising, but opening our own studio would not be a good investment.

Although working in DC for a large organization provided opportunities to learn and to advance professionally, it also showed me more about the political environment – internally and externally. During my time at the headquarters office, I think we had many different Chairmen, and they each put their own Executive staffing in place. I felt that I had advanced as far as I could in the current environment, and I wanted to find a position that was not so tied to the political environment in DC. So, I resigned without having another job in place. I wasn't quite as stupid as this implies because I made my effective date six weeks in the future. I was lucky; I found a position as a Vice President in charge of Residential Lending at a Northern Virginia bank.

I again had to earn the respect of the employees. They resented me because I came from a large DC organization. They did not respect me or the position I held. I gave everyone a fair chance to perform, but if the employee didn't perform, I cleaned house. I became known as the hatchet lady. It was not my intent to earn that designation; it was my intent to lead the department in achieving its organizational goals for employee growth and organizational profitability. I was in charge of originations, secondary market operations, closing, post closing, investor reporting, and loan servicing, and I quickly saw that changes needed to be made and new procedures needed to be put in place. Mortgage-backed security trades were done on little slips of paper; there were no automated loan or loan sale systems; there were no written policies and procedures; and there was no quality control system. I changed all of this. I led a project to develop automated loan tracking and secondary market systems, brought in Moody's for a rating for bulk sales, developed written policies and procedures, developed a quality control system, created teams to process loan sales, developed bulk sale packages, and created relationships with industry investors. In doing this, I wanted staff to understand why they were doing things a new and different way or why they needed to consider alternatives in solving problems. In discussions where there were options to consider, I often supported the side I did not think was the best option; it helped me see the alternatives better. I was particularly proud when my staff practiced before coming into my office for a discussion. One of my managers told me I was the hardest supervisor she had ever had but that I was also the fairest. I held celebrations after large loan sales, and it became the norm that when we had loan sales coming up, everyone wanted to participate on the team. But this did not happen overnight, it took me a while to gain their respect and to create a team environment. Not everyone was a fan, but I don't think any boss has everyone as a fan. I had one young underwriter who just didn't like me. But my biggest obstacle was my direct reporting relationship. I had a dual reporting responsibility when I first came – to the Senior Vice President and to the President. The Senior Vice President was good in making deals but did not seem interested in the operational side of the business. That is why I was hired – to manage the operational side of the business. The Senior Vice President did not like it that I was also taking orders from the President, and in fact, called me into his office one day with one of the staff members that reported to him in attendance and told me, "I will bring you to your knees." He ultimately resigned, and I was promoted to his job. When I achieved this promotion and became part of the executive team, the "good ole boy network" was still prevalent. At first, I tried to assimilate and be one of the boys, but I soon realized that what I needed to do was to earn their respect and have them accept me as an equal and as a female. Once this happened, I respected my colleagues more, and I think they respected me for who I was. Although some women used their femininity to help them gain positions, this path did not guarantee that they would be respected for their abilities. I worked hard to improve the attitude and respect for professional females in the workplace, and I am troubled today when I see professional women who don't continue to model what women like me worked so hard to achieve.

I was running and competing in 5k, 10k, and ten-mile road races, and training for the Richmond Marathon with my sister. Becky ran with me some; and Sharon and I often met halfway between our houses in Richmond and Northern Virginia to train. When I say I "competed," I use the term loosely because I was only competing to improve my time, finish the race and not be last. I kept my running shoes in my office in case my staff wanted to send me out for a run if they found my mood getting disagreeable. I injured my knee two weeks before the Richmond Marathon,

> Ode to Helen in Celebration of Her Birth
>
> "You ran through the wall and remained on your feet, you kept right on going – said "the hell with de-feet.". You finished the race with great pride and a smile. You've run through your life in a similar fashion, in play and in work, you do all with great passion.
> In one single month you managed a lot --
> Senior VP, 50 years and a long trot".
>
> Poem from two colleagues when I became SVP, ran the marathon and turned 50 – Susan and Carole

and I was devastated. I did everything I could to rehabilitate my knee, but I couldn't so I started training for the Marine Corp Marathon the next year. My children were my support crew during my training runs, but during the Marathon, there was a much larger support group, including friends and my sister and her family. I trained often with Shelly and Rodd (her husband to be). Of course, they ran much faster than I did so it was their easy run and my hard run. The three of us completed the Marine Corp Marathon, and we celebrated my 50th birthday at the finish line.

My Mother had relocated to Richmond to live with my sister Sharon after Daddy died, and I had an opportunity to get to know my Mother differently than I had known her as a child. She was much stronger than I had thought. She was young at heart, and a lot of fun! She had surgery for cancer when she lived in Brownsville, and it came back. She was hospitalized the last several weeks of her life. Sharon and I took turns staying all night in the hospital with her, and we were both with her the night she died. While she was in the hospital, I left work on Thursday and came back Monday evening, and I did not give my work a second thought during this time – family was first. This was one of the hardest things I had done – along with being there for my Dad at the end too. But Sharon was always there with me, and these are times that we shared that could not have been shared with anyone else.

I had good relationships with my senior management colleagues at the bank, but when there were changes being made that affected one of my colleagues (he was being replaced without his knowledge but everyone else seemed to know about it), I felt I could not work in an organization that would treat an employee this way. The particular employee had been with the organization for at least 20 years. Again, I had no job to go to, and I had funds that I left on the table if I had stayed. I have never put economic considerations above personal integrity, but looking back, it may be misplaced pride. I don't know.

I had changed houses several times by now. First, moving to a larger and nicer town house, then to another condo and finally to an older house in another county west of the northern Virginia area.

Becky had eloped, after having moved to Virginia Beach to be near her husband-to-be who was in the Navy. We all helped her move, and Jo and I even drove for about three hours to pick up a cushion from her couch that had fallen off one of the pickup trucks  that was carrying all her worldly possessions. Her husband, Rob, was subsequently stationed in Florida, and her first child was born there. Jake had moved to Florida after graduating from high school so he was in Florida, and Shelly, Jo, and I all came down the week before she was due; but unfortunately, she was a little late delivering so only Jake and I were there, along with Rob, her husband, of course, for the delivery. Becky completed her undergraduate degree and was the first and only one who completed her degree so we had a celebration to honor her and her

accomplishment. By this time, both Becky and Jake were back in the DC area and were there when Shelly got married.

Shelly was married on a beautiful day in October, and it was the best wedding I have ever attended. She and her husband paid for most of it, and Rodd's Mom and I contributed a little. But it was a pricey wedding (although wonderful), and Shelly and Rodd were still paying for it a couple years later. They made it theirs. Rather than a traditional wedding dance, they broke into a tango and had all those in attendance clapping and laughing.

After resigning from the bank, I obtained a couple of consulting contracts, and I took my examination to become a real estate agent. Nonetheless, I was not making enough money to maintain my lifestyle. I had spent the retirement I received when I resigned my position, and after months of struggling to keep my head above water, I had to file Chapter 7 bankruptcy. This was very difficult for me, and is one of the things I have done that I am most ashamed of and embarrassed about having done. It was totally my own doing, and it didn't have to happen if I had managed my money better. But it did, and I had to accept the consequences.

About the same time, I connected with a former colleague from Fannie Mae. In fact, he had been my boss, and we met to establish our own consulting firm. We worked well together, and made a couple hundred thousand dollars our first year. But after spending about six months on one contract, neither of us felt like we were being true to the business plan that we had structured while hiking in the mountains. One of the most important features of the plan was keeping a balance between work and family, and this wasn't happening. So, we dissolved our partnership. I had enough income from my partnership to put funds down on a small cabin in the mountains, which I did. The total price for the cabin was less than $40,000 so it was quite small. It did have a wonderful screened in porch that was where I spent most of my time.

After these events, I realized that I needed to think about what I really wanted to do professionally. I had always been interested in older adult issues so I applied to graduate school at Virginia Commonwealth University to seek a Master degree in Gerontology. I moved to Richmond and lived in an apartment above a garage. I obtained a position at the Rehabilitation, Research and

Training Center at VCU. I worked in supported employment helping students with disabilities transition to the workplace. One particular project that I developed as a part of a grant on supported employment was still operational last time I checked. It involved a collaborative relationship with the school system, hotel management, and social services. I still remember the students I had fondly, and I learned a lot while employed in this capacity.

I then obtained a consulting job that I could work on remotely, so I moved back to my cabin and took online courses for my Masters. After that assignment, I found a job in Hilton Head, SC and relocated there since I could continue my school work online. First, I worked for a rental company but then quickly found a position in a continuing care retirement community. I worked in the Maintenance Department and learned a lot about the issues that faced the residents in the various sections of the development. I became friends with one woman who was blind and visited her several times to read to her and just to have good conversation. She was a very interesting person, and I enjoyed knowing her. She cooked for me one evening, and I kept in touch with her after I left. I was sad when one of her relatives contacted me after I moved away to tell me she had passed away.

I came back to Northern Virginia to finish my Masters and to start looking for a job in my new field once I completed my degree. I lived in my cabin again and found two part-time jobs making $5.15 an hour to support me. I got up at 3:30 in the morning, drove 45 minutes to open a sports club, and then went to work at a car rental agency in the afternoon. Whether I was making $5.15 or $150 an hour, I gave the same quality of work.

My first job after I got my Masters was with the NAHB Research Center, on a grant-funded project on senior housing. My responsibilities were primarily to research and write reports, and I did not have an opportunity to use my management skills. But I learned much and was happy to have an opportunity for a position working in my second career area. It can be challenging to start at the bottom in a new career when you have been at a high level in a previous field. I have always believed that management skills can transfer easily from one field to another, but this does not seem to be shared by many organizations – especially if the candidate is a female.

I did not know what kind of position I would be best at in the field of Gerontology so I was interested in exploring the possibilities. My role at the Rehabilitation Research and Training Center had given me the opportunity to do some hands on and project development work in the disability area. My responsibilities at the Research Center were primarily research and report writing in the field of aging and housing. The next opportunity I had was with a local Area Agency on Aging – again at a lower level. I was in charge of two areas within the agency – employment for low-income seniors and a tax service program. This gave me an opportunity to work directly with consumers but also to utilize my program development skills. I expanded the employment program to serve all older adults, regardless of income and held a conference attended by over 100 people that provided information and presentations to aid in the job search process, and the tax program received a state award. But the most rewarding experience occurred while attending a soccer game for my grandson, and a woman came up to me and said, "Hello Helen, do you remember me?" I recognized her as one of the people I had helped find a part-time position. She told me that I had helped her to achieve what she had today. The part-time position that I helped her find led to a permanent position. Then she was able to move out of her daughter's house. She had her own apartment and in addition to working full-time, she was doing some volunteer work. Wow – that made me feel good!

In continuing my job exploration process, I applied for a position with the AARP Foundation, and I was hired to manage a grant-funded project. This appeared to be a position that would enable me to use my management skills along with my project development skills in a way that no others had thus far, and I liked it. This was a two-year grant so at the end of the project, I again looked for another position, and by now, I realized that I was better at the management level even though it was rewarding to work directly with consumers. Next, I found a position with the National Association of Area Agencies on Aging. I started out managing the national call center that provided information and resources to consumers and subsequently progressed to Chief, Programs and Communications Officer in charge of all grants and programs. This was a good match for my skills and experience. I enjoyed working at the organization, and I liked having multiple projects. I had a new idea a day – some not good—but every once in a while, I had a good one. We brought the Call Center in-house, obtained a grant for a volunteer Center, expanded our activities in community living, and reached out to new partners. The CEO was very supportive, and I stayed with the organization until I retired. One of the things I did learn was that there seemed to be more internal politics in the non-profit field than what existed in the corporate field. Perhaps it was a difference in time. But I could resolve the details of a $40 million bulk loan sales contract over the phone with my word in the corporate field, whereas in the non-profit sector, it took much longer to negotiate partner responsibilities on a million dollar grant. Perhaps I never achieved the same level of respect in the non-profit field that I enjoyed in the corporate field. I don't know.

When I retired, I thought I was done, but I was wrong. I didn't want to quit work completely so I did one consulting project. I learned something else about myself. I need to keep busy and feel like I am contributing. I have done some volunteer work but not on a regular basis. The kind of volunteer opportunities where I live do not fulfill my need to contribute to the broader society. I am keeping my eyes and options open. Tomorrow is a new day…

CHAPTER 14 – THE GYPSY IN ME

I love to move! And I love change. This drives my family and some of my friends crazy. I don't know why I do. Perhaps it's because I like the struggle or it could be genetic. My Dad was a merchant marine and traveled the world, but he never really told us about it. I wish he had or I wish I had asked.

I have lived in many houses – I rented some and owned others. Sometimes, I had both a rental house while I owned a house. Below is a list of houses I lived in after I was divorced.

Apartment1, Atlanta, GA

Apartment 2, Atlanta, GA

Townhouse Apartment, Atlanta, GA

Town House in Glen Cove, Northern Virginia

White House, Northern Virginia

First Town House, Burke Center, Virginia

Second Town House, Burke Center, Virginia

Condo, Burke Center, Virginia

Flint Hill House, Virginia

Cabin, Winchester, Virginia

Apartment, Hilton Head South Carolina

Apartment, Solomon's Island, MD

Apartment 1 above Garage, Richmond, VA

Apartment 2, Above Garage, Richmond, VA

Apartment near Museum, Richmond, VA

Log Cabin House, Lovettsville, VA

Apartment, Alexandria, VA

Townhouse, Alexandria, VA

Condo, Woodbridge, VA

Apartment, Delray, VA

Condo – Torpedo Factory, Alexandria, VA

House, Alexandria, VA

Carriage House, Purcellville, VA

House, Round Hill, VA

House, Clarksville, VA

I list my housing detail to illustrate that I truly do love to move, experience new and interesting environments and meet new people.

My moves were usually necessary because of economics or jobs. The first move to Georgia was for a job. The second two were economic. One was because I needed to move to a less expensive apartment; the other was because I could afford to move to a better townhouse apartment. The move to the first townhouse in Northern Virginia was for a job. The move to the White House in Northern Virginia was because I had enough money to rent a house. The move to the log house in Lovettsville was for a job as was the move to the apartment in Solomon's Maryland. There were a few, however, that were just because I was tired of living in one environment and wanted to live somewhere new. I am reminded of this by my daughter, Becky. This was the primary reason I moved to Hilton Head, SC. In fact, my usual timeframe to live in one house was two years, and my son-in-laws wanted to get me blow-up furniture because they had to move me so many times.

I always looked for apartments or houses that had character or were located in interesting areas. When in Hilton Head, the apartment I rented had the Sound on one side and the ocean on the other. When I came home from work, I often walked along the beach with the dolphins that were only a few yards away. Hilton Head was also a great place to run. I had courses mapped out all over the island. My moves weren't all bad for my family since they gave them fun places to visit -- like Hilton Head and Solomon's Island, Maryland.

I like to travel and have taken spur of the moment trips, even with my young children. When we lived in Atlanta, I decided one day to go to Savannah for the weekend so we just packed our bags and took off without making a reservation at a hotel. I knew we would find something.

I like to interact with the local people when I travel. When I traveled for work, I tried to make an effort to learn something about the local area and eat at local restaurants. I frequently drug colleagues with me on these excursions. One time, when a colleague and I were doing a training seminar in North Dakota, one of the participants lent us her car so we could drive to the Badlands.

I've been to the Atlanta and London Olympics. My daughter, Shelly, has been to both with me. When my daughter Jo moved to the U.K., a completely new group of travel options opened up for me. (She went to the Olympics in London with Shelly and me.) For a while, Jo and I would take a trip during Thanksgiving, and when my daughter Shelly started traveling routinely internationally for her job, we were able to combine some trips with her. My daughter Becky is always up for any new adventure (could she have some gypsy in her too?). Jake likes adventures and the peace from being outside. He often shares pictures with me from his early morning motorcycle rides.

One year I arranged for all of us to spend Christmas in the U.K. with Jo and then to go to Spain for a couple of days. Not all of the grandchildren were there, but Jake and his wife, Diana, came with their young daughter. I think she was only a year and one-half at the time. I have been to Italy three times, Paris a couple of times, Wales once, the U.K. many times, and Spain three times. In fact, I have been back to Spain twice for a month with my

granddaughter, Kaitlin. This has been a very special time for us. We stayed in the same apartment in the residential area in Marbella, Spain, went to familiar restaurants and cafes, and hiked the five-mile boardwalk between Marbella and Puerto Banus each trip.

We also became very familiar with the bus system. We could go anywhere within the city and nearby towns. I love Marbella!

Some suggest that the frequency with which I have changed houses and my love of travel shows lack of ability to settle or a restlessness on my part. I don't know ... Perhaps I am just hopelessly curious.

CHAPTER 15 – GROWING OLD

I am growing older every day, and I am sure my experiences are not that different from others. But having said that, I do know that our aging experiences, although similar, are unique just as we are. Some of the changes that have happened to my physical body, mental capabilities, and to my spiritual and emotional feelings are not bad. Some I manage, some I accept, although sometimes not gracefully, and others I still ponder how best to deal with them.

My emotional responses also seem different as I age. I have become more sensitive. I remember when I was doing a presentation several years ago, being mocked by two young women in the audience and who gave me a poor evaluation. I was in my 60s at the time, and I could not determine if what they found offensive was my personality, the manner in which I made the presentation, my age, or if they just thought I did not know the subject matter. Perhaps it was all of these things. One of the responsibilities that I believe we have as adults is to set good examples. I feel this responsibility keenly and try to set good examples in all aspects of my life –family, work, and play. So, I wonder how the behavior of these two young women was a good example for others; or was it just bad manners. I talk about this example because I think, as I have gotten older, I am more susceptible to being hurt by negative criticism than I was as a younger person. Perhaps other older people are too. I am also less likely to be as critical of others. I keep saying, "I've mellowed." Perhaps this mellowing happens to many of us as we age. Also, I appreciate the little things more now. When I see a young baby, I smile. Looking out the window yesterday, I saw a bluebird. That made me smile. Receiving a phone call from family or friends makes me instantly happy. A couple of weeks ago, I walked in the state park near my house. That made me happy too.

I have always felt a connection with Hans Margolius's poem but even more so as I age.

"Whoever is easily susceptible?

to the troubles and cares

of life is equally susceptible

to the joys that life has to offer."

The challenges to my physical body are ongoing as I grow older. Some are interesting. When I look at my aging skin "hang" on my bones, I think that is unattractive so I wear tops that cover the top part of my arms. When I see wrinkles on my face, I don't mind them so much, because I think of what my daughter Jo told me years ago. "It looks like someone lives there."

I have more of a problem with the health-related changes that prevent me from doing some of the physical activities and exercises that have always been an important part of my life. I have had to learn to manage multiple health issues as I age. I'm glad they didn't happen all at once, or it would have been overwhelming! I was first diagnosed with a low platelet count (ITP) of unknown origin in my early 50s. That was scary, but because we weren't sure whether I would still be able to run, I took up hiking. Through hiking, I met wonderful hiking friends that I still have today and have enjoyed many hours on the trail with them. In fact, we did two long-distance hikes that are special to me – the Dogwood Half Hundred (no longer a hiking event) and the C and O Canal Hike. For the Dogwood Half Hundred, my family and friends supported me as they always have on my exercise events. My daughter Shelly hiked the last six miles with me, and carried my hiking stick. My friend Barbara gave me her shirt because I was too hot in the shirt I was wearing. Barbara also hiked part of the trail with me; and at one point said, "I'd tell you to look down to see how pretty it is below, but don't because you might fall." (It was the latter part of the long hike, and I was tired by then.) Becky, my daughter, and Kaitlin, my granddaughter, were there to encourage me and to give me water at one of the last stops.

When I hiked the C and O Canal with three of my hiking friends, Sabra, Janice, and Edy, I was very excited because we hiked part of the trail after dark with flashlights, and this brought back my camp days. I enjoyed many training hikes with my hiking friends before and after these two events that are fond memories still. So, my being diagnosed with a  low platelet count gave me these experiences and friends that I might not have had.

One of my hiking friends and I decided to take rowing lessons in Old Town, Alexandria; it was something I had always wanted to do. I liked it so much that I continued rowing after those initial lessons. One of my favorite things was to be on the Potomac with the moon still visible, and the sun starting to rise, hearing the oars all click together in the oarlocks, the paddles hit the water at the same time, and seeing our nation's capital in the background. I am in awe that a little girl from Indiana could have this experience. But one morning, as we were racing in a four-man boat, I just couldn't seem to keep rowing. I was very tired and short of breath. At the insistence of my daughter, Becky, I went to the doctor and after being referred to a Pulmonary Specialist and Cardiologist, I was diagnosed with Idiopathic Pulmonary Fibrosis and mild Pulmonary Hypertension. There is no cure for Pulmonary Fibrosis, but just recently, two new medications are showing positive results for possibly slowing the progression of the disease. Although predictions for life expectancy after diagnosis range from two to seven years, I have had pulmonary fibrosis for 11years. I have been fortunate, but I have always kept exercise in my life even though I can no longer run (or jog at a pace that others would call running or jogging or do hills unless I go very slowly), but I continue to exercise four or five days a week at a minimum.

I had a flare-up with the fibrosis a couple years after diagnosis, and I was put on oxygen when I exercise and when I fly. Therefore, I purchased a portable oxygen concentrator with assistance from my daughter Shelly for use when I fly and exercise. I have purchased three other concentrators since then and have tried to use them jogging/walking outside, but I haven't found one yet that works that well outside. Nonetheless, I continue to listen to my body and maintain an exercise program, some without oxygen and some with oxygen. I have also been fortunate to have a pulmonary doctor who listens to me and is comfortable when I don't follow the pattern of how doctors generally follow pulmonary patients. I only see her when I need to. I told her once that I consider myself an athlete, and she said, "You are."

My other chronic condition is Bowen's Disease or multiple squamous cell skin cancers. I had been going to a Dermatologist for years for the occasional basal or squamous cell cancers, but my visits became more frequent as growths were found more frequently. The most serious was a recurring squamous cell on the top of my head that had been removed once with Moh's procedure. When it came back, I was sent to an otolaryngologist because there was a depression near the site that seemed to suggest involvement with a bone. I ended up in Sloan Kettering having surgery and a skin graph. But right before my scheduled surgery, I woke up with shingles! So my surgery had to be delayed a week. I don't usually think that things bother me much, but apparently, the prospect of surgery did more than I thought! Luckily, the bone was not involved, but I continue to go to Dermatologist for monitoring. So, I wear a hat, use lots of sun block and find shade to walk in outside, but I still go outside. I adapt.

I have been fortunate throughout my life. My children and sister have supported me in my exercise endeavors but also during my health adventures. Becky and Shelly were with me in the hospital after my surgery, and Jake came up from Georgia to drive me to New York for one follow-up appointment with my doctor. Sharon came down to stay with me for a few days after I came home from the hospital. And I am not an easy patient to be around as I am sure all my children will confirm. But I don't think this behavior is new to being old. I just have more opportunities to display it now.

I was also diagnosed with osteopenia or osteoporosis many years ago, but I did not opt to take any of the medicine since in my mind, the research did not provide enough support for the value of taking the medication.

After managing all of these conditions for a number of years, I thought I was done having new conditions; I was wrong. When I went in for a routine eye exam, I was diagnosed with Central Retinal Vein Occlusion – again idiopathic. The standard treatment is shots in the eye, but I asked the doctor whether it was possible that it could get better on its own. Although he said not likely, he did say it was not an unreasonable approach to take for a month. This is what we did, and low and behold, my condition has steadily improved, and now I just have to be checked to make sure it doesn't recur. Whew!

So while I resent having these physical conditions, I can manage them and have in fact, found new and positive activities and friends because of them. I take no medications, and I have been able to adapt to the changes. As I get older, every day is an adventure with my physical body. If I overeat, eat the wrong foods, don't sleep enough, over or under exercise, or if I am overly stressed, my body spanks me so I have to listen more intently to my body as I age.

On the other hand, I find some of the mental changes that take place amusing. Sometimes I hear words come out of my mouth that I have no idea where they come from. I also seem to be more cautious about things than I was when I was younger. I tell my children that when these words come out, to just ignore me. I don't mean them; "I am just talking like an old woman. "

Furthermore, I sometimes find myself more in a hurry. I am typically a high-energy person, but sometimes I wake up with an agenda that I can't wait to get started doing. Perhaps because I realize that I don't have that much time left to do them. I finally realize that there are things I won't have the time or the physical capability to do. I don't know whether I will be able to do a triathlon, but I haven't completely given up on it. I don't have a pool nearby or flat roads to jog on, but then again, that could change. I could move again! But even if I can't make this dream come true, there is still much I can do. I just have to be more realistic in what I can achieve. I can write this book. I can start a non-profit company (which I'm beginning to work on). I can exercise. I can support my family emotionally. I can plan reunions. I can be a good friend. I can read good books (and some bad ones too if I want to). I can laugh out loud. I can travel. I can volunteer. I can enjoy being outside. I can learn to play the piano, a foreign language, and more. These are just my current interests. I can continue to try to be a better person, and most of all, I can continue to be an active participant in this world so long as my physical and mental capabilities let me. I just have to remember to listen to my body.

I have become more introspective as I age. I don't know whether this is good, bad, or any different from how other older adults feel. I am amazed at what other people in previous times thought and wrote when my words and thoughts seem very similar to theirs. I love many of the philosophical writings of Thoreau, Emerson, and Einstein. They inspire me and make me happy.

I also think more about what will happen when I die, and I would be lying if I didn't say I was a little afraid. Even with a strong faith, we still can't know for sure what will happen. As I age, I challenge myself about my faith. Do I practice the faith that I purport to believe. I have never been comfortable talking to others about my spiritual faith, except to say I believe in a higher power. I believe in the goodness of people and trying to be good to those less fortunate. I have been blessed in my life with the happiness and opportunities I have been given. I know others have not been so fortunate, and I know it is up to us to try to make it better for others less fortunate. I have not been as good at this as many other people have been. And for this, I am sorry. I wish I were more giving of myself, but I know that we all have different capabilities and opportunities so I have accepted me for who I am. My question to myself is should I be doing more to live my life in a manner consistent with my beliefs. I'm still working on this.

When I think about dying, what I mind the most is leaving family and friends and a world that I think is wonderful. But one thing I know is that we will all die, and somehow that is comforting to me. I don't think dying will be bad. It's like completing a favorite book that you don't want to end. Sometimes, we imagine continuing the characters in the book in new directions, and I think that's how death will be. I just don't know what adventures await. Right now, I'm just grateful when I wake up in the morning without a new itch, ache, or pain.

EPILOGUE

So now what? Throughout this book, I've written about issues relating to "Community," "You," and "Me." I hope reading through these Parts will motivate you to tell your own stories and to examine your views about social practices that affect you and your community. At times, writing this book has been a struggle because I am not a writer. The 15 years it took me to write it will attest to that!

But I have felt driven to write it as my example of telling my stories and thinking about how those stories contributed to my values. So, I hope that those of you who read this book will find some reason to think about your stories and your values. If you do, I will have succeeded in my purpose. I hope you do.

I know nothing but …

INDEX OF PHOTOGRAPHS

20527601R00068

Made in the USA
Middletown, DE
29 May 2015